THE SECRET OF LAUGHTER

BY

ANTHONY M. LUDOVICI

Author of

A Defence of Aristocracy
Woman: a Vindication
Man: an Indictment
etc.

CONSTABLE & CO LTD
LONDON

first published 1932

PRINTED IN GREAT BRITAIN BY
MACKAYS LIMITED, CHATHAM

THE SECRET OF LAUGHTER

PUBLISHED BY
Constable and Company Ltd.
LONDON

·

Oxford University Press
BOMBAY CALCUTTA MADRAS

·

The Macmillan Company
of Canada, Limited
TORONTO

PREFACE

ALTHOUGH, in effect, a new theory of laughter has emerged from the present essay, this was not so much its original object as was the fresh investigation and vindication of a very old theory of laughter which, so it seemed to the author, had too consistently been given scant justice especially by Anglo-Saxon scholars, writers and critics.

If the reader will only agree to examine this old theory afresh under the author's guidance, it is hoped that he will find, not only that it has been too hastily set aside as inadequate, but also that the discoveries made in the closer consideration of its merits have provided the basis for a more comprehensive and therefore more satisfactory explanation of the phenomenon of laughter than has yet been achieved.

Those who are familiar with Darwin's *Expressions of the Emotions in Man and Animals* will remember that in the chapters of the book in which he deals with the question of laughter he was evidently at great pains to dispel the popular and scientific belief that laughter is a purely human expression. As an evolutionist, he was naturally more puzzled than a non-evolutionist would have been by the fact that laughter should suddenly have made its appearance in Man without leaving any traces of its gradual development in those higher animals most closely related to him. To meet the difficulty he therefore advanced one or two somewhat unconvincing reasons for believing that laughter was actually found in certain higher animals, reasons which I cannot help thinking are based upon the incurable anthropomorphism of the class of men from whom he obtained some of his information.

The theory expounded in this book, however, makes the evolution of laughter perfectly clear, and accounts quite satisfactorily for the fact that, as an expression of joy and pleasure, it should be found only in Man.

This is an age in which laughter and all the means of provoking it stand very much higher than they have ever stood before in public esteem, more particularly in Anglo-Saxon countries. It can hardly be said, therefore, that the subject is uninteresting or untopical ; and, seeing that hitherto no satisfactory and all-embracing theory of laughter has been discovered, it is hoped that, in spite of its many unpalatable aspects, and the many idols it demolishes, this new theory may be given at least the serious consideration which has been accorded to many of its predecessors.

The author has carried the theory about in his mind for many years, lecturing upon it and discussing it with all sorts and conditions of men. But it was only after wide reading, mature reflection and the careful consideration of much bitter criticism received from audiences at lectures, scholars, psychologists, offended humorists and, above all, women, that he decided to record it in book form, as hitherto it had seen the light only in a brief outline published in *The Referee* of December 30th, 1928. The first suggestion that the theory of laughter here fully expounded should be made accessible to a wider audience than any the author could hope to meet at lectures and debates, was made by the members of the English Mistery, before whom a paper on the *Secret of Laughter* was read by the author on December 8th, 1931.

London,
    May, 1932.

INTRODUCTION

It is strange that an age like the present, which is so clamorous in its demand for humour at all costs and on all occasions, should know so little and trouble so little about the nature of laughter.

Guided by their newspapers and their modern books, the average man and woman (particularly the latter), without any idea or thought of what laughter really is, cling tenaciously to the view that humour is good and desirable, and, what is more, unquestioningly assume the right of making the most damaging remarks about people who lack it, and the most laudatory about people who possess it. In fact, during the Great War, when the journalists had exhausted the last dregs of invective against the German Kaiser, and cast about them for some final and annihilating insult that would express the ultimatum of their own and their readers' loathing and contempt of him, you will remember that they could think of nothing worse than to accuse him of having no sense of humour. And the Anglo-Saxon world rejoiced, because it imagined that this finished him much more effectively than did the revolution in his own country.

The fact that this view of humour, like most popular views on other subjects, is the outcome of the modern standardisation of opinion, and that the majority of people adopt it without knowing how or why, does not prevent the average man and woman (particularly the latter) from displaying every sign of resentment and anger if, to their faces, you question its validity. And from the bitterness and fervour with which they defend humour when its extreme desirability is questioned, you might almost be led to believe that each individual in modern society had independently and by his or her own original effort arrived at the conclusion that humour is a good thing. It is one of the marvels of modern standardisation that those persons seem to be the least aware of it who are its most humble victims.

A moment's independent and original thought would have led these unconscious victims of standardisation to the conclusion that, quite apart from the meaning of laughter itself, humour was, on its own account, a problem of some complexity, and that it was therefore precarious to concede too hastily that it was necessarily good. For instance, it would have occurred to them that true and passionate lovers are not humorous. If they are thwarted or rebuffed they refuse to see any humour in the situation. In fact, the very ability to look humorously on a situation of this kind would render the depth and sincerity of their passion suspect. This does not, however, prevent the modern world from urging young people to show more humour when they happen to be in such a situation. It would also have occurred to these victims of standardisation that no great creator, teacher or world-builder has ever been a humorist in the modern sense, and that if a modern English or American humorist had been at the elbow of such a man, the usual exhortations to be humorous at all costs would have completely crippled all hope and desire to do anything epoch-making.

Imagine a modern English or American humorist at Luther's elbow at the beginning and during the progress of his struggle. He would have addressed the German reformer more or less as follows : " My dear, good fellow, are you sure you are not taking yourself and this Protestant stunt of yours much too seriously ? It's all very well ; but just show that you have a sense of humour, don't be so damned certain that you are right, don't be so ridiculously earnest, and you'll find that you'll be able to laugh at your present intensely comic gravity, and the world will laugh with you instead of at you."

And nothing would have been done.

But Luther had no modern English or American humorist at his elbow. He therefore took both himself and his mission intensely seriously, and displayed such a total lack of humour that when he stood before his judges all he could exclaim was, " Here I stand. I cannot act otherwise. God help me ! "

Likewise, if Napoleon had had a modern English or American humorist at his side when he left Egypt and embarked on that gigantic enterprise, the reconstruction of anarchical, bleeding and devastated France, he would hardly have dared to say what he did say. He would have been obliged at least to pretend that he saw both sides, that he recognised the overpowering disproportion between his absurdly inadequate personality and the stupendous task he was undertaking, and he would have had to crack some paralysing joke about it.

Instead of this, he said, " I am going to France to drive out the lawyers." And he did !

Thinking on independently and originally, the victims of thought standardisation would, moreover, have discovered that there is not a joke in the whole of the New Testament, that even the laughter of the Bible is nearly always an expression of scorn and not of mirth (exceptions : Psalms cxxvi, 2, and Job vii, 21), and that no saint,[1] prophet or apostle is ever spoken of as laughing.

They would have discovered that Christ is everywhere in deadly earnest, taking himself and his mission most seriously, and expecting to be taken seriously, and that if he had not been so serious, if he had fulfilled his mission as many modern reformers have thought fit to fulfil theirs, we should have forgotten all about him to-day, just as we shall have forgotten all about them to-morrow.

True, Mr. Chesterton, that typical modern and humorist, could not rest in peace while Christ, the all-perfect Being, continued to be regarded as deficient in the most exalted of modern Anglo-Saxon virtues—a sense of humour. To him it seemed almost blasphemy to withhold from the Perfect One this latest hall-mark of perfection. In his book *Orthodoxy*, therefore, he corrected Christ's orthodox biographers, and to his own intense satisfaction and that of all his equals, expressed the considered opinion that if Christ is not reported to have laughed, it was because he deliberately hid his mirth from men. He was capable of it, *of course !* But he covered it " constantly by abrupt silence or impetuous isolation." And thus Chesterton restored to the Founder of Christianity that quality which had obviously been omitted from the list only by mistake, by an oversight. Christ had a sense of humour after all, and everybody heaved a sigh of relief ![2]

How much more reverent and more indicative of a profound understanding of laughter is Lamennais' protest : " Who could ever imagine Christ laughing ? "[3]

This extreme example of the modern worship of humour ought surely to have aroused suspicion. But it did not ! It merely confirmed all Mr. Chesterton's readers in the belief that humour was eminently desirable.

Truth to tell, there is in every inspired and passionate innovator a haughty energy which is incompatible with the cowardice and indolence of humour. As, however, this cowardice and indolence in humour are not immediately obvious, the matter must be examined more narrowly.

What strikes the foreign visitor to our shores most forcibly is that with but few exceptions, such as a religious service, there is now hardly a ceremony or an assembly where humour is not *de rigueur ;* so much so that an after-dinner speech has come to be regarded merely as a means of provoking laughter, and some people—one very well-known London figure among them—reduce the convention to an absurdity by standing up and reciting one after another a whole string of anecdotes, which have no more connexion with the objects of the society giving the dinner, or with the special interests of the diners, than if he had picked them at haphazard out of a book. I have been at innumerable dinners where there was only the flimsiest pretence of making a relevant speech. Everybody, including the chairman, merely racked their brains for one or more anecdotes and proceeded to recite them until the lateness of the hour alone brought a welcome end to the dreary business. Illuminating or merely interesting and sustained discussions of any topic or subject of general or even particular moment are almost unknown outside the learned societies, and even they indulge in interesting talks only when they meet for business.

In private houses no remark is listened to that does not provoke a laugh or a smile, and to attempt to enquire into any political, social, artistic, scientific or moral question, except in a flippant and irresponsible way is considered the worst possible form.

It is here suggested that, quite apart from the meaning of laughter, cowardice and indolence lie hid in this convention—*cowardice* in the speaker, because to be earnest and vehement on any question of moment may excite derision *without forestalling it* (a terrible experience for the vain modern man), and in both the audience and the speaker, because it requires more courage to face a question squarely and to deal with it seriously than to treat it frivolously and flippantly ; and *indolence* because, if the convention were, as it should be, that people must talk interestingly and helpfully or not at all, there would have to be either much more silence than there is, or else much closer consideration of the questions concerning which most people claim to hold opinions. Humour is, therefore, the lazier principle to adopt in approaching all questions, and that is why muddle is visibly increasing everywhere. Because the humorous mind shirks the heavy task of solving thorny problems and prefers to make people laugh about them.

In the public and professional modern humorist, however, the vice of cowardice becomes so deeply interwoven with his technique of appeal, it is so essentially a part of his stock-in-trade, that the wonder is that more people are not aware of it. I refer, naturally, only to those public humorists who attract attention, and wish to attract attention, by dealing with questions of great moment to humanity.

To come forward with ideas, either of reform or of iconoclastic novelty, is dangerous and unpopular. Crucifixion, spiritual or physical, ostracism, or at least hatred, is the popular reaction. The man who does this seriously and earnestly, stakes his life, or at the very least his prestige, on the undertaking. If he is not stoned, crucified, driven beyond the pale, or starved, he may be laughed at, jeered at, guyed! Nothing lends itself more readily to ridicule than passionate earnestness. But those men whom we associate with lasting and fundamental reforms in the past, risked all this. They risked crucifixion, the stake, the block, everything, even being laughed at!

But your modern humorist reformer is a coward. He wants things both ways. He longs for the laurels of the epoch-making reformer and iconoclast, he hankers after the reputation of the deep and earnest thinker, but his vanity shrinks, not so much from the thought of naked exposure on the cross, or in the stocks, but from—laughter !

This is a risk he refuses to run. He therefore *forestalls* laughter. He makes it his business to convince his hearers that he is not in earnest. He advances with his weighty proposals in his mind, but with a broad smile on his lips and, if possible, a laugh and a fool's cap ready to hand, before he attacks his thorny problems. If, therefore, the crowd laughs, it is because he wishes them to laugh. He has commanded their laughter. Consequently he cannot be the victim of it.

This is the new type of saint, prophet and sage. It is an Anglo-Saxon invention. But a new Anglo-Saxon method of keeping alive the memory of these new saints, prophets and sages will have to be invented also, for posterity will never be able to remember them by anything they have achieved.

There are, however, other peculiarities about humour which might puzzle the victims of standardised opinion if ever they thought independently about it. By studying recent history they would have discovered that as fast as the clamour for humour has swelled the quality of national achievement has depreciated, muddle in national affairs has increased, the stamina of the nation has declined, and the spectacle of national glory has become retrospective rather than contemporary. They would have discovered that, in the days when Englishmen still had so little sense of humour that they kissed each other and wept in public, there was more manliness, more independence, and above all more self-reliance in the country than there is to-day. Finally, they would have discovered that because men have a sense of humour nowadays, and consequently never dream of taking themselves or their convictions or their desires or anything that is theirs very seriously, they are exceedingly easy to lead and to control, and that this accounts for the ardent and irrational attachment to humour displayed by almost all Anglo-Saxon women. The man with a sense of humour will always climb down; he takes nothing, least of all his authority, seriously; consequently, if his wife very much wishes to tread on him, as she generally does, she finds that she meets with no determined resistance. Nobody fires up more angrily than the cultured Anglo-Saxon woman when she hears the sense of humour attacked. Without in the least understanding the reason for the general worship of humour, she knows very definitely that she is defending one of the first prerequisites of her power, her dominion. She has two most effective bludgeons with which to stun her menfolk into docile stupor if ever they stand seriously and firmly by one of their opinions or desires. The one is to accuse them of selfishness (this, owing to abuse, is beginning to lose its coercive power), and the other is to question their sense of humour. This immediately secures subjection, because no modern man can suffer this accusation to remain hanging over his head.

Quite apart from the meaning of laughter, then, it is obvious that all is not as absolutely clear as it might seem about this matter of humour. Not that I mean to imply that humour has no place in social life, or has not its immense value as a recreation and sometimes a refuge. I merely question the desirability of its ubiquitousness to-day, and suggest that its extraordinary vogue is in need of some explanation. There must be some reason, even apart from that advanced in regard to women, why the clamour for it should be so universal and unabating.

At all events, even if we dismiss all the above considerations as of no consequence, we still cannot be satisfied that humour is so eminently desirable, in season and out of season, whether in discussing grave or frivolous matters, unless we know something about the meaning of laughter and of the condition people are in when they demand laughter as insistently as it is being demanded to-day.

To discover the meaning of laughter and its evolution, as also to ascertain the condition mankind is in when it demands laughter with such neurasthenic insistence as it does at present, is the two-fold object of the following chapters.

CHAPTER I

I AM going to suggest that there is something sinister in laughter. But by this I do not mean that it is necessarily bad. Many very desirable things have either had sinister beginnings, or else have their sinister side. Nevertheless, when we know the sinister side of laughter, although we may not, like Henry I., dismiss it for ever from our gamut of expressions, at least we shall be in a position to understand its function and the meaning of the present high esteem in which humour is held.

Before I concentrate on the main theme, however, I should like to illustrate my use of two terms—" superior adaptation " and " unconscious " by a few examples.

In the *Battle of the Frogs and the Mice*, which some have ascribed to Homer, a mouse, stopping on the bank of a pond to drink, is invited by a frog to pay him a visit. The mouse consents and mounts the frog's back to go to the latter's castle. In the middle of the pond, however, an otter frightens the frog, who dives, and the mouse is left to drown. Now, from the moment the mouse mounts the frog's back, it is the frog, in spite of his inferior position, who enjoys, as compared with the mouse, superior adaptation in

B

the sense in which I am going to use the term in this book.

In La Fontaine's fable of *The Fox and the Stork*, you will remember that a fox invites a stork to dinner and offers the food in two flat platters, from which he alone is in a position to eat the food. By way of retaliation the stork then returns the invitation and offers the food in two narrow-necked vases into which he alone can introduce his long, slender beak. At the first meal it is the fox, and at the second the stork, who enjoys superior adaptation in the sense in which I propose to use the term.

A man who has only one glove in a company of people all of whom have their complement of gloves, a man who is left on the pavement in the rain to wait for the next omnibus while those in front of him fill the one that has just driven up, and a man who loses his hat in the wind while those about him do not—each of these men is in a position of inferior adaptation, while those about him, or in front of him in the case of the omnibus, enjoy superior adaptation in the sense given to the term in this book.

The term " unconscious " I shall use in the sense usually meant when people speak of blinking by an " unconscious " reaction when an arm or stick is suddenly raised in front of them. The sense in which I propose to use it is also well illustrated by an incident in Charles Reade's *The Cloister and the Hearth*. There, one of the male characters is tracked down by spies to a certain inn. But they find that the only guest at the inn is a woman. One of them, suspecting that the woman is really a man in disguise, tries the ruse of flinging a coin into her lap, and from the spontaneous closing of her knees (a reaction that would not be spontaneous in a woman accustomed to skirts and the obstruction they would offer to a falling coin) he concludes that the woman, as he suspected, is really a man in disguise. The spontaneous closing of the knees was the man's " unconscious " response, in my present sense.

Now one of the main difficulties in investigating the meaning of laughter consists in the great variety of circumstances in which a laugh seems a suitable expression. For instance :

(*a*) A small child, hard pressed by a pursuer, laughs when it reaches safety in the folds of its mother's dress. There is nothing obviously funny or humorous, however, in running to safety.

(*b*) A young woman, knowing herself to be well dressed, smiles constantly, and laughs at the slightest provocation. There is nothing obviously funny or humorous about being well dressed. On the contrary, it is often more funny and humorous not to be well dressed.

(*c*) We are told that the gods on Olympus burst into loud laughter when they saw Hephæstos hobbling lamely from one to another offering them nectar. Hephæstos was the crippled ugly god.

(*d*) We are told that David Garrick once broke down in a tragic scene because he was laughing so much at a man in the front who, owing to the heat, had placed his wig on his dog's head.

(*e*) Children and some adults laugh to see Harlequin belabouring the clown.

(*f*) Some people laugh to hear other people speaking a foreign language, or speaking their own language in an odd way. Much of the success of Harry Lauder in London was due to this human peculiarity.

(*g*) Many people have difficulty in not laughing at someone who loses his hat in the wind and proceeds to grope about for it, at great personal risk, under the bonnets of cars and the heads of horses.

(*h*) On the other hand, that same person will laugh while he is trying to recover his hat, and will look anxiously and laugh at those near him when he first loses it.

(*i*) Once on a damp, greasy day, in Old Bond Street, where the pavement has two different levels, a smartly-dressed woman, evidently unfamiliar with the two levels, fell in front of me. Her handbag dropped on the flags and sprang open, money rolled in all directions, and I noticed that her white gloves, her silk stockings and the skirt of her dress were badly soiled. And yet, the whole time that I and a few others assisted her to her feet and helped her to recover her property, she never once stopped laughing. Now it cannot be funny or humorous to fall and soil one's clothes in the street.

(*j*) We laugh when we inhale nitrous oxide.

(*k*) We also laugh at a mere absurdity, as, for instance, when we are told that two lions, kept in adjoining cages, broke through the partition separating them, and in their fury mauled each other until only the tips of their tails were left.

(*l*) Again, the more dignified the person is who has a fall, the more we laugh. A ragged, bedraggled

20

tramp falling in the dust or mud is not nearly as funny as one of His Majesty's judges, or a bishop performing the same antic.

Sydney Smith, writing over a hundred years ago, gives a curious instance of this. He says :

" If a tradesman of a corpulent and respectable appearance, with habiliments somewhat ostentatious, were to slide gently into the mud and decorate a pea-green coat, I am afraid we should have the barbarity to laugh. If his hat and wig, like treacherous servants, were to desert their fallen master, it certainly would not diminish our propensity to laugh. . . . But if instead of this we were to observe a dustman falling into the mud, it would hardly attract any attention."[1]

(*m*) We never laugh at a horse, a child or an old woman who falls.[2]

(*n*) We laugh when we are embarrassed. In fact, the typical mannerism of all timid and ill-adapted young people on the stage is a perpetual simper or laugh.

(*o*) We laugh at any mishap that may occur to a performer on the stage. Voltaire actually said : " I have noticed that a whole theatre audience never laughs loudly as one man except when a mishap occurs to one of the performers."[3]

Once, I believe it was at the Coliseum, I saw Sir Frank Benson walk on to recite a speech from one of Shakespeare's historical plays. He was in the garb of some ancient knight or noble, and as he approached the footlights he tripped over his long sword. The whole audience rocked with laughter, and although he bravely shouted the speech he had to deliver, nothing would compose the house to seriousness, and at last he had to retire discomfited.

(*p*) We laugh at schoolboy howlers. But—and this is most important—we only laugh if the howler is one which our own unaided knowledge enables us to recognise as such. When we hear a schoolboy refer to the bridge spanning the Menai Straits as a " tubercular bridge," we may laugh. We may also laugh when we hear him describe an oculist as a fish with long legs. When, however, the howler concerns some science or language with which we are not familiar, we cannot laugh, except out of courtesy to the interpreter, even when the howler is carefully explained to us. Why is a mistake we know of our own knowledge to be a mistake, funny, and a mistake we know through someone else's knowledge to be a mistake, not funny?

(*q*) We laugh at a pun.

(*r*) We laugh more heartily and loudly at a joke or a pun in a foreign language, which we happen to understand, than at a joke of equal merit in our own language. De Quincey[4] thought that many scholars had, as the result of a like infirmity, grossly exaggerated the value of certain classical writers.

(*s*) We laugh when tickled.

(*t*) We smile or laugh when we meet a friend. But even when an enemy passes and we are in company, we also take care to smile or laugh, to indicate to the enemy that we are no worse off for his absence from our circle.

(*u*) Although a joke may be really funny, we rarely if ever think it so if it is against ourselves.

22

An instance of this occurred at the Law Courts a few years ago, in the case of Captain Wright *versus* Lord Gladstone.

Mr. Norman Birkett, counsel for Lord Gladstone, cross-examining Captain Wright, said : " Did you see the daily papers on July 28th ? " Captain Wright said : " No."

Mr. Birkett suggested that the reading-room of the Club would contain all the London daily newspapers —he could have seen them there.

Captain Wright retorted : " I am a journalist, not a barrister. I don't rush to the papers to see if my name is in them."

There was some laughter and Mr. Justice Avory remarked : " There is nothing funny in that."[5]

Evidently some people present did think it funny. Mr. Justice Avory could not, however, because, being a member of the legal profession, and having been a barrister, he could not enjoy a joke which exalted journalists at the expense of the dignity of his own calling.

(*v*) When we slip in trying to reach a platform, or knock our heads by accident in front of a crowd, we provoke loud laughter ; but it offends us to be laughed at. Even animals, according to some people, are annoyed at being laughed at.[6]

(*w*) We laugh at a surprise, or an expectation that ends in nothing. Many investigators have believed this kind of laugh to be the only kind.

(*x*) We laugh at an incongruity (Schopenhauer's example under (*k*)).

(*y*) We laugh at a good nonsense picture by Lear or Bateman.

(*z*) We laugh at mere caricature.

(*A*) We laugh at disguises.

(*B*) We laugh when others laugh.

(*C*) We laugh at a good ruse, a good trick, a good case of diamond cut diamond, and at a witticism.

(*D*) We laugh at good mimicry or imitation.

(*E*) We laugh in what we conceive to be an intellectual way, when, in a public debate, one disputant cracks a joke against his opponent, and we then regard the disputant who has had the joke cracked against him as defeated in the argument.

(*F*) We laugh at mere indecencies, or at scenes, reference and stories actually indecent, bordering on the indecent, or reminiscent of the indecent, on the stage, in books, and in daily life.   Men, after dinner, when the ladies have retired, habitually laugh at indecent and salacious stories.

I have now given thirty-two examples of laughter, in which the expression is associated with different circumstances.   There seems, at first glance, to be very little connexion between these various laughs—between, for instance, the laugh of embarrassment, the exaggerated laugh at the joke in a foreign language, and the laugh provoked by nitrous oxide ; but seeing that all the examples I have given provoke the same expression—laughter—it would seem that some common factor must connect them, and that if we find this common factor, we shall know the nature of laughter and what causes it.

I have deliberately omitted the laughter of hysteria and the laughter of insanity resulting from the methodical feet-tickling which is alleged to be a form

24

of torture among the Chinese. This I did because both are morbid, and not enough is known about them to enable a description of the mental processes involved to be made. The abuse of a normal reaction in the case of methodical and persistent feet-tickling may or may not lead to insanity ; but if it does it would have no more to do with normal laughter than the production of tears by the stimulus of a freshly-cut onion has to do with normal weeping. It would come under the head of mechanical stimulus and purely mechanical reaction, it would not interest us as enquirers into the nature and function of laughter as a social expression, and would be explained along the lines of Herbert Spencer's *Physiology of Laughter*. As to hysterical laughter, we know that it is commonly associated with sex-repression or sex-starvation—hence the implied sex-connexion in the name. But whether the hysterical fit of laughter is provoked by an exalted state of mind, by a consciousness of increased power, or not, we do not know. I suspect that it is.

It is obvious that unless we can discover an explanation or definition of laughter that will account for all the kinds of laughter I have enumerated, it will not be an explanation or definition at all. Even to leave one example of normal laughter out would suffice to ruin the definition.

What has been done by thinkers and philosophers in the past about the matter ?

CHAPTER II

For a very long time, from the days of Socrates and Plato, the thinking world of Europe has been perplexed by the problem of laughter, the variety of the occasions for it, and the uniformity of the reaction in this variety. To enumerate all the theories that have been advanced about it, I should require a whole volume. But there is no point in thus duplicating work that has already been admirably done by others. In both Mr. Kimmins' *The Springs of Laughter*, and Max Eastman's *The Sense of Humour*, excellent summaries will be found of the various theories of laughter through the ages. Suffice it to say, therefore, that, roughly speaking, ever since the days of Plato there have been two schools of thought on the subject :

(*a*) The school of those who treat the matter superficially and think, as most ordinary people do, that there is no mystery and nothing sinister about laughter, and,

(*b*) The school of those who go into the problem more deeply and think that, on the contrary, there is a mystery in the phenomenon of laughter and that it has its sinister side.

Of the authors and thinkers who see no mystery in laughter or who, in any case, regard it either as wholly delightful and innocent, or at least as compatible with a moral order of the universe, the most important are :

Sir Philip Sidney, Lord Bacon, Pascal, Voltaire, Sydney Smith, Smollett, Kant, Hegel, Byron, Hazlitt, Schopenhauer, Dickens, Carlyle, Professor Lipps, Emerson, Spencer, Ribot, Camille Mélinaud, Renouvier, A. Penjon, Dewey, Bergson and Freud.

Lord Bacon is singularly jejune. He says : " In laughter there ever precedeth a concept of something ridiculous,"[1] which amounts simply to saying that laughter is the expression provoked by the laughable. He adds that " the object of it is deformity, absurdity, shrewd turns and the like," but this is to state merely a fact of common experience without explanation.

Pascal and Sir Philip Sidney sought the cause of laughter in a surprising disproportion between what one expects and what one sees. " Laughter almost ever commeth of thinges moste disproportioned to ourselves, and nature," said Sir Philip Sidney.[2] He certainly added that it " hath only a scornful tickling," and that " we laugh at deformed creatures," and " at mischaunces." But here again, although the field is wide, he gives us merely the facts of common experience, and without a particularly good generalisation. He seems, therefore, to belong more to the present than to the next section dealt with in Chapter III.

" Nothing makes people laugh so much as a surprising disparity between what they expect and what they see," said Pascal.[3] In his eleventh *Provinciale*,[4] he also says that laughter can be a weapon for social discipline, and, therefore, that it may inspire fear and shame. But all this is too limited and leaves entirely

27

out of account all the purely subjective states which may provoke laughter, to mention only one grave omission.

Voltaire, who is quoted with great satisfaction by all whose chief concern it is rather to defend laughter and humour from any taint of " self-glory," than to discover what it really is, says : " Some men have argued that laughter is born of pride and that people imagine themselves superior to those they laugh at. True, man is a laughable creature ; but he is also a proud creature. Pride, however, is not a cause of laughter. A child who roars with laughter does not indulge in this pleasure because he sets himself above those who make him laugh."[5]

This, which is probably a thrust at Hobbes, and a most foolish one, because, as we shall see, Hobbes's " self-glory " is very much more profound than Voltaire suspects, is to state the case against the less superficial views of laughter, not merely with a lack of candour, but also with either the conscious or unconscious intention of confusing the issue. Because, although we may be compelled to agree with Voltaire so far, that a feeling of pride is not traceable in all laughter, we know that pride does enter into some laughter, and we also know that a child sometimes laughs out of pride, although not necessarily out of pride towards those " who make him laugh."

Besides, we are still without any satisfactory explanation from Voltaire as to why the child, or anybody, laughs at all, or at anything in particular. To say, as he does, that " in laughter there is always an element of joyfulness incompatible with contempt and indignation,"[6] is again unfair and deliberately confusing. For, although laughter may be incompatible with " indignation," it is certainly not incompatible with " contempt." Moreover, where is the mere " joyfulness " in the laughter of embarrassment, the laughter of surprise, and the laughter over schoolboy howlers, which only comes if we can of our own knowledge recognise them as such ?

If all laughter is joyfulness, then it seems as if Voltaire has merely given us another name for laughter. For in the three examples just mentioned, if the laughter is merely joyfulness, everybody must see that it is not a sufficient explanation, and that behind the joyfulness, there must be something provoking it. Consequently we are still in search of the ultimate provocation of laughter.

Like Sydney Smith, below, Voltaire seems to have been either not quite candid, or else not quite clear about laughter ; because he knew and admitted that what Sir Philip Sidney called " mischaunces " could also provoke laughter. He says : " I have noticed that a whole theatre audience never laughs loudly as one man except when a mishap occurs. . . . Harlequin only makes us laugh when he makes a mistake."[7] And he adds : " I have never heard people roar with laughter, either at the theatre or in company, except in cases similar to those I have mentioned."[8]

Very well, then, Voltaire acknowledges that these " mischaunces " happening to our fellows (not only on the stage be it noted, but also " in company ") were the cause of the most hearty laughter he ever heard. How did he reconcile this with his contention that laughter, being only joyfulness, is incompatible with a sense of superiority?

Nobody would claim that *all* laughter is provoked by " mischaunces " happening to our fellows ; but since Voltaire himself regards the example he gives as that which provoked the heartiest laughter ever heard by him, it is curious that he should still have been able to reconcile it with his generalisation.

Sydney Smith, not unlike Pascal and Sir Philip Sidney, sought the cause of laughter in the opposition of ideas, in " incongruity which excites surprise " and " *only* surprise " ; and, in the example quoted from him above (under *e*) he says we laugh at the tradesman in " habiliments somewhat ostentatious " who slides down gently into the mud, because the opposition of ideas is great, and we do not laugh at the dustman, " because the opposition of ideas is trifling and the incongruity so slight."[9]

He goes on to say, " Incongruities, which excite laughter, generally produce a feeling of contempt for the person at whom we laugh. I do not know that I can state an instance of the humorous in persons, when the person laughing does not feel himself superior to the person laughed at. . . . In all such cases the laugher is, in his own estimation, that superior man ; the person laughed at, the inferior." But although this seems to get very near a more profound understanding of laughter, one feels that Smith believed that it is the incongruity still that causes laughter, and not the self-glory. This, if I read Smith correctly, he regards merely as an accompaniment of the laugh caused by incongruity. In fact, Smith, like Voltaire, is muddled. He sees elements in laughter incompatible with his generalisation based on incongruity ; but retains the generalisation notwithstanding.

Both Pascal and Sydney Smith, however, like Voltaire, fail to explain many of the examples I have given above—for instance, the laughter of embarrassment, the smile or laughter over schoolboy howlers, when we know of our own knowledge they are howlers, and many others.

Yet another group, to which Hazlitt, Hegel, Schopenhauer, Lipps and Camille Mélinaud belong, see the cause of laughter in incongruity. According to Hazlitt, " the essence of the laughable then is the incongruous, the disconnecting one idea from another, or the jostling of one feeling against another."[10] But among the instances he gives of the laughable, many are very far from being merely innocent contrasts. Moreover, he says : " Someone is generally sure to be the sufferer by a joke. What is sport to one is death to another. . . . The injury, the disappointment, shame, and vexation that we feel, put a stop to our mirth ; while the disasters that come home to us, and excite our repugnance and dismay, are an amusing spectacle to others. The greater resistance we make, and the greater the perplexity into which we are thrown, the more lively and piquant is the intellectual display of cross-purposes to the bye-standers. Our humiliation is their triumph."[11]

To have been able to say and admit all this, and still to have clung to his generalisation, justifies me, I believe, in placing Hazlitt, with Smith and Voltaire, among those who treat laughter superficially.

According to Lipps, the laughable is " a descending incongruity in which our attention passes from great things to small,"[12] a view in which he concurred with Kant and Spencer, on whom he bases it. And, according to Camille Mélinaud, " when from one point of view a thing is absurd, while from another it occupies a definite place in a familiar category, our thought experiences, as it were, a sudden shock—this is laughter."[13]

Schopenhauer says : " The cause of laughter in every case is simply the sudden perception of the incongruity between a concept and the real objects which have been thought through it in some relation."[14] Among the many examples he gives to illustrate his theory, is the following : A guard of soldiers once allowed a man who was their prisoner to join them at a game of cards, and because he cheated them, they kicked him out of the guardroom ; that is to say, they set free a man whom they were supposed to keep in custody.[15]

Hegel, whom Schopenhauer loathed more than any other man, does not deal nearly as thoroughly with laughter as his junior did, and like most of the men in this section, seems to regard the question as not important enough for careful treatment. He says : " On the whole, it is extraordinary what a variety of opposite things excite human laughter. Matters of the dullest and most vulgar description will move men in this way ; and often they laugh quite as heartily at a thing of the greatest moment and profundity, provided only that some important feature of it becomes apparent, which is contrary to what they are used to,

and to what they commonly believe.   Thus laughter is
merely the expression of self-complacent shrewd-
ness, and a sign that they, too, are clever enough to
recognise a contrast, and to feel above it.   There
is also the laughter of mockery, scorn, despair,
etc."[16]

Apart from the fact that he acknowledges an element
of superiority in laughter—superiority as the result of
having recognised a contrast and being above it
—Hegel seems to associate himself with those who
think an incongruity or contrast is the cause of laughter.   But he makes no attempt to connect this laughter
with that of mockery, scorn and despair, or to show
how the same expression can do duty on so many
different occasions.

The ten men above mentioned are hardly more
helpful than Bacon and we have only to compare their
definitions with the thirty-two examples of the laughable we have given to see how seriously inadequate
they are.

To Immanuel Kant[17] and Herbert Spencer[18]
laughter is the result of an expectation, which, of a
sudden, ends in nothing.   This, too, is not nearly
exhaustive enough and fails to include many of the
most common and frequent causes of laughter.

Emerson inclines both to Schopenhauer and to
Kant and Spencer.   He says : " The essence of all
jokes, of all comedy, seems to be an honest or well-
intended halfness ; a non-performance of what is
pretended to be performed, at the same time that one
is giving loud pledges of performance.   The balking
of the intellect, the frustrated expectation, the break of

C   33

continuity in the intellect, is comedy, and it announces itself in the pleasant spasms we call laughter."[19]

This, too, is quite inadequate.

Carlyle, in his pretentious and shallow little book, *Sartor Resartus*, makes no attempt to define laughter, but speaks of it generally with such whole-hearted approval and such spiteful condemnation of those who do not laugh with great resolution and noise, that the unwary reader is tricked into believing that here is something more than bogus profundity or superior claptrap.

" Readers who have any tincture of psychology know . . . that no man who has once heartily and wholly laughed can be altogether irreclaimably bad . . . the man who cannot laugh is only fit for treasons, stratagems and spoils ; but his whole life is already a treason and a stratagem."[19a]

So superficial and yet so plausible ! In any case, it lent the authority of a grossly-overrated writer to the popular view of laughter, which we also find reflected in the works of Dickens, Smollett and Byron. A most exceptional woman, George Eliot, succeeded, as we shall see, in making a much better and closer shot at the truth ; but owing to the fact that a certain shallowness is essential for wide popularity, George Eliot's view of laughter is not nearly so well known as Carlyle's, nor has it a hundredth part of the latter's influence.

The next group, consisting of C. Renouvier,[20] A. Penjon, and John Dewey, see in laughter a sort of release from constraint, an attainment of liberty. Penjon thinks laughter is the expression of liberty, a release from the constraints of rationality. But apart from the indefatigable reiteration of this idea in different keys, there is little either helpful or convincing in his essay on the subject. He says, for instance : " The smile with which one hails a friend, which accompanies and sometimes replaces a few words of greeting, or the smile of a man who has finished a difficult task, likewise constitutes the natural expression of an increase of liberty."[21]

It is difficult to agree with Penjon in all this. His first example is badly chosen. I myself have suggested (under (*t*) in Chapter I *supra*) as an example of laughter, the laugh or smile with which we greet a friend. But how this is to be connected with an increase of liberty, I fail to see. It is easier to see liberty in Penjon's second example.

Speaking of the regularity of daily, civilised life, with its science and conventions, he says : " On the other hand, everything that interrupts this regular process, this uniformity, provided that it does not frighten or injure us, or cause suffering to anybody, makes us laugh, or feel inclined to do so."[22] There is something in this ; but it does not cover all laughter by any means, and when he adds : " Laughter seems to be the result of a sort of shock caused by the sudden disturbance of a uniform sequence, already observed and expected to continue,"[23] he seems to be closing his eyes to a good three-quarters of the common causes of laughter.

He certainly admits an uncharitable element of superiority in some laughter ;[24] but even this does not make him relinquish his inadequate generalisation.

Professor John Dewey regards laughter as the

sudden relaxation of a strain, the attainment of unity after a period of suspense or expectation. This obviously limited and wholly one-sided view of laughter will not do ; but it has the quality which all definitions so far have had—that is, it allows laughter to leave the dock without a stain on its character.

Dewey is, however, helpful, because at least he sees that humour is not the only or even the chief cause of laughter. " A very moderate degree of observation of adults," he says, " will convince us that a large amount of laughter is wholly irrelevant to any joke or witticism whatever." But apart from that, his view that laughter is the sign of a " termination of effort," i.e., that it is like a sigh of relief, and is the expression of doffed gyves, is palpably inadequate. " The laugh," he says, " is thus a phenomenon of the same general kind as a sigh of relief," and he adds : " Both crying and laughing fall under the same principle of action —the termination of a period of effort."[25]

Ribot, like Cicero, gives up the definition of laughter as impracticable. He says : " Laughter is the outcome of such a variety of different causes—physical sensations, joy, contrasts, surprise, eccentricities, unfamiliarity, low behaviour, etc.—that it is doubtful whether a common basis can be found for them all."[26]

We now come to Bergson, probably the most respected of the modern contributors to the subject of laughter, and in any case the man who has made the most painstaking and most earnest attempt to solve the problem.

Bergson's treatment of the subject has two aspects :

(*a*) the actual definition of the laughable, and (*b*) the function of laughter.

(*a*) Stated briefly, Bergson sees the laughable in any manifestation of the living human being—whether on the physical or the spiritual side—that betrays a tendency to be inelastic, rigid, or mechanical, that is to say, in which matter seems not wholly animated or successfully controlled by the spirit, and where adaptive ease gives place to mechanical stiffness and awkwardness. As an example on the physical side, Bergson says : " A man, running along the street, stumbles and falls ; the passers-by burst out laughing. They laugh because his sitting down is involuntary. Consequently it is not his sudden change of attitude that raises a laugh, but rather the involuntary element in this change—his clumsiness. He should have altered his pace, or avoided the obstacle that threw him. Instead of that, through lack of elasticity, as a result, in fact, of rigidity, the muscles continued to perform the same movement when the circumstances of the case called for something else. That is the reason of the man's fall and also of the people's laughter."[27]

On the spiritual side, unconscious repetition or absence of attention, as revealed in an unintentional play on words, makes us laugh, because the author of them is behaving like an automaton, instead of consciously like a living, thinking animal. Thus the deliberate play on words causes a laugh because of its connection with the involuntary play.

This fits in magnificently with Bergson's *Evolution Creatrice*, in which he expounds his system of the universe ; but it is unfortunately wholly inadequate, and were it not for the hopeless confusion that prevails in this subject of laughter, it would never have been given a second thought. How about the laughter of the child running to safety ? The laughter of the lady who fell in Bond Street ? Our laughter at schoolboy howlers provided that, of our own knowledge, we can immediately recognise them as such ?

Truth to tell, Bergson's view of laughter is among the most restricted and inadequate, although he wrote a whole book to explain it. Had he been less anxious to light on a theory fitting his fundamental view of the universe, I cannot help thinking that a man of his ingenuity must have found a more comprehensive theory. The fact that his theory of laughter has met with such widespread approval, at least in England, is easily accounted for if we remember :

(1) The high esteem in which humour is now held, and (2) the consequent desire that everyone feels to see laughter explained as innocently and as pleasantly as possible.

(b) But it is when he comes to explain the function of laughter that Bergson reveals most superficiality and most thoroughly deceives both himself and his readers.

According to Bergson, laughter is a sort of disciplinary chastisement, a form of social ragging, a means of making people conform to the conventions and rules of society, and a weapon against anti-social or eccentric conduct. Thus the function of laughter is that of a lash which makes nonconformists smart.

All this is most ingenious, and a rather superficial writer in the magazine *Psyche*, S. Edwards by name, waxes so enthusiastic and eloquent about it, that he completely forgets himself and claims that Bergson found " an explanation that will cover all instances of the comic," and that he " goes to the very foundation of things."

And yet the whole of Bergson's theory of the *function* of laughter as a form of social chastisement for unsocial conduct depends upon laughter itself having in it, on occasion only, an element of scorn and contempt. If it is *sometimes* a lash, how and why and when is it a lash ? You may exclaim, " Oh, but we all know it is that ! " Yes, but why ? Unless we know why, we have not only failed to explain laughter itself, but we have also failed to explain how it can fulfil this supposed social function. The fact that it does not always fulfil it, and that, times out of number, laughing has no such function, ought to have made Bergson pause. But although he speaks of the fear[28] laughter inspires, and admits that it is always humiliating for the person laughed at,[29] nowhere does he begin to explain how or why it inspires fear or is humiliating. Had he done so, he would necessarily have arrived at a much more profound and comprehensive theory of laughter itself.

Because this element of scorn in laughter, because the reason why laughter inspires fear and humiliates and may therefore be used in a disciplinary fashion,[30] is not touched upon by Bergson—a fact that does not in the least disturb the writer in *Psyche*—his whole theory is left, as it were, hanging in mid-air.

Not only, therefore, is Bergson's explanation of the laughable inadequate, but his definition of the function of laughter is also built upon an assumption, which he does not even see as an assumption. He takes for granted, like thousands less philosophical than himself, that laughter can be an expression of scorn and can inspire fear, without once showing how or why, or asking himself how or why.[31] There are a large number of such assumptions in Bergson's philosophy.[32]

Freud is chiefly interesting, not as a guide to the meaning of laughter, or as a discoverer regarding its function, but rather as a psychologist who enriches our knowledge of the possible thought processes preceding certain perceptions of the comic. As might be expected, he makes much of the return to the infantile state in laughter and in the production of adult wit, and tries to show that while wit pleases because it is derived from an economy of expenditure in inhibition, the comic because it is due to an economy of thought, and humour because it arises from an economy of feeling, all these three economies really take us back to the infantile beginnings of mind, when states of unembarrassed and unconstrained pleasure were common without the need of the artificial stimulation of wit, the comic and humour.

This is helpful since it takes laughter away from the object and back to the subject in a way that the other theories do not. But it hardly says enough about laughter itself, as a gesture and an expression. In some respects Freud approaches Spencer in the theory of static psychic energy finding a free vent in laughter, and both Spencer and Kant in the theory of the laughable being a descending incongruity ; while, in that part of his theory in which he emphasises the element

40

of relief—particularly the relief from critical reasoning —he inclines to the views of men like Renouvier, Penjon and Dewey.

Apart from the valuable hint regarding the state of the subject in laughter, however, we feel after reading *Wit in its Relation to the Unconscious* no nearer an exhaustive definition of the laughable or to an understanding of the deeper meaning of laughter itself as a gesture, than we did after an examination of all the previously enumerated theories.

Those who see in laughter no harm or mystery, therefore, are not very helpful. Each of them lights on some aspect of laughter which all of us know quite well; but none of them gives us a comprehensive theory or even a hint of one. We do not laugh only when we are confronted by an incongruity, a contrast, an expectation that ends in nothing, a human being's resemblance to a machine, a human being's unsocial conduct, or by a mental state recalling childhood's euphoric and irrational condition. But the most inadequate and false of all the views of laughter quoted above is surely that of Carlyle, who, with his usual blend of bombast and spite, is definitely misleading.

CHAPTER III

TURNING now to the philosophers and authors who do not think laughter so harmless, and who attempt to explain it in a manner less superficial than the previous set, we find the more important are :

Plato, Aristotle, the author of the *Coislinian Treatise on Comedy*, Demetrius, Quintilian, Plutarch, among the ancients ; and among the moderns, Descartes, George Herbert, Thomas Hobbes, Spinoza, Swift, Addison, Montesquieu, Lord Chesterfield, Oliver Goldsmith, Lamennais, Stendhal, Darwin, George Eliot, Alexander Bain, MacDougall, Professor Lloyd Morgan, Dr. Wrench.

I do not suggest here that every one of these people gives us a comprehensive definition. Many of them are as one-sided as the former set. But at least they avoid the banality of seeing in the laughable merely such abstract states as a contrast, an incongruity, or a surprise ; at least they have the profundity to see that laughter is not and cannot be always an entirely harmless and innocent expression, and they all belong by right to the line which culminates in a complete and comprehensive explanation of laughter, whether as an expression or as a social function.

In the *Philebus*, Plato discusses laughter with some care and the upshot is that self-ignorance is the cause of the ridiculous.   This self-ignorance, however, whether in a vain conceit of beauty, of wisdom, or of wealth, is ridiculous only if those who are guilty of it are weak ; it becomes detestable if they are powerful.[1]

This is merely an elaborate way of saying that the foibles of those who are too feeble to injure us are merely funny ; but that the foibles of those who are strong enough to injure us may prove to be our tragedy and are therefore a matter of grave concern for us.

In the *Republic*, Plato deprecates laughter very much as Lord Chesterfield does, at least among people of quality ; for he says that the guardians of an ideal state are not to be given to laughter.[2]

Elsewhere in the *Republic*, and again in the *Laws*, he speaks of the things that should not, and those that should be, laughed at.   In the former, he says : " He is a fool who thinks anything ridiculous but that which is evil, and who attempts to raise a laugh by assuming any object to be ridiculous but that which is unwise and evil."[3]   And in the latter he says : " About serious matters a man should be serious."[4]

This is the first hint we get in antiquity that all is not well with laughter, and there is in it something against which it is advisable to be on one's guard. The general impression derived from Plato is that there is always a contempt of something or somebody in laughter.

In the *Poetics*, Aristotle takes the idea a stage farther and makes it more precise.   He says : " The ridiculous is part of the base or ugly.   It is the kind of failing and deformity which does not cause pain or disaster, such

43

as one may see, for example, in the comic mask. This is ugly and distorted without being painful."[5]

Again we get the idea of something mean and contemptible behind the comic, that is why Aristotle, in the *Rhetoric*, is able to define wit as "educated insolence."[6] And this view of laughter recurs all through Greek and Roman writers.

While valuable as constituting the first step in the direction which sees something not altogether innocent in laughter, the views of Plato and Aristotle, however, miss a good deal. For instance, they offer no explanation of that purely subjective cause of laughter which comes insistently to the human creature who feels at the top of his form, and who, standing in the sunshine, is free and unburdened by cares ; they offer no explanation of the laugh of embarrassment, of safety, or of the exaggerated laugh over a joke heard in a foreign language which we happen to understand.

The author of the *Coislinian Treatise on Comedy* either follows Aristotle's theory, or directly represents it. He says, among other things : "The joker will make game of faults in the soul and in the body."[7]

Demetrius of Alexandria also derives the ridiculous from some deformity, and follows Plato in warning the prudent to laugh only at opportune times—at feasts, symposia, and in rebuking luxury and high living.[8]

Cicero, although dismissing the definition of laughter as impracticable, follows Aristotle in believing that "laughter has its basis in some kind or other of meanness or deformity ;"[9] and Quintilian, while approving of this view of Cicero's, also points out that "sayings designed to raise a laugh are generally untrue (and

44

falsehood always involves a certain meanness), and are often deliberately distorted, and further, never complimentary."[10] He then adds that " laughter is never far removed from derision."[11]

In Quintilian's statement we see the element of contempt in laughter extended so as to include not merely deformity, defectiveness and ugliness, but everything that may be " uncomplimentary " to a human being ; but in the *Questiones Conviviales* almost all the occasions for laughter mentioned by Plutarch refer to physical or moral defects.[12]

There is in these ancients too much stress on the purely reactive laughter resulting from a plain and unmistakable appeal to the laugher's sense of physical superiority, and we feel that a number of the commonest causes of laughter in cultured adults are being overlooked ; but it is more candid and helpful to acknowledge this factor in the laughable as important and even basic, than to attempt to deny it altogether as some over-anxious modern defenders of laughter are wont to do.

Among the moderns, Descartes was probably the first who troubled to explain the physiology, or the bodily mechanics of laughter. In this, however, he is naturally not very helpful, though he has interesting things to say about laughter itself. " Although apparently," he says, " laughter is one of the chief signs of joy, it is only moderate joy, in which there is a mixture of admiration and hatred, that can give rise to it."[13]

And again : " Experience also teaches us that in all those cases which give rise to that hearty laugh which comes from the lungs, there is always a slight element of hatred, or at least of admiration."[14]

Descartes is obviously puzzled by the complexity of laughter. Although he sees a tincture of hatred or admiration in it, his language on the subject is not positive and does not suggest that he was satisfied with his attempted solution. He leaves the problem very much as a writer might leave an unfinished essay —intending to take it up again—just roughly sketched out. But what makes him interesting is that his rough sketch has most of the essentials in it, and would have required but very slight modification in order to develop into a sound finished structure.

George Herbert, writing in 1631, expressed emotionally a sensitive man's doubts about laughter. He probably felt, just as Bergson did,[15] that the attitude of mind in laughter is at root inconsistent with charity and ideal justice ; but having no system into which laughter had to be fitted, was able to say so outright, without circumlocution, or explanations which confused the issue.

> " Laugh not too much," he wrote, " the witty man
>   laughs least :
>   For wit is news only to ignorance. . . .
>   All things are big with jest ; nothing that's plain
>   But may be witty, if thou hast the vein."[16]

An important point is made here, which is that the humorous or funny side of all things is only too obvious to most men of culture, and constantly to call attention to it—to make it *de rigueur* to call attention to it—is the pastime of lesser minds.

It was, however, not until 1651—that is to say, about two thousand years after Aristotle had first pointed the way—that the world was given an explanation of laughter, which, in its depth and comprehensiveness, not only included the doubts of a Herbert, the groping suspicions of a Descartes, and the clear, if one-sided, vision of the ancients, but also supplied a place for a kind of laughter—that laughter which may be called subjective and which arises from an inward and not an outward stimulus—to which, with but one exception, no place is given by any writer before or after.

Thomas Hobbes is a very much underrated thinker. So little trouble has been taken to do him justice on this point of laughter alone, that whole chapters and books have been written against him by men who have not even taken the pains to consider " subjective laughter " as an important aspect of laughter, and who have not even once referred to it in their discussion of the subject. So angered have they been by their own hasty and narrow reading of his meaning, and so anxious have they felt to rescue laughter from his hands, that, just as Puritans can deal with life only by amputating and limiting it, so they are able to deal with laughter only by shutting their eyes to many of its most important aspects.

I shall now quote Hobbes, and if the reader will bear with me, I hope, in the sequel, to be able to show how completely satisfactory and therefore comprehensive his explanation is.

" There is a passion," says Hobbes, " that hath *no name ;* but the sign of it is that distortion of the countenance which we call *laughter,* which is always *joy ;* but what joy, what we think, and wherein we triumph when we laugh, is not hitherto declared by any. That it consisteth in *wit*, or, as they call it, in the *jest*, experience *confuteth ;* for men laugh at mischances and indecencies, wherein there lieth not wit or jest at all. And foreasmuch as the same thing is not more ridiculous when it groweth stale or usual, whatsoever it be that moveth laughter, it must be *new* and *unexpected*. Men laugh often, especially such as are greedy of applause from everything they do well, at their *own* actions performed never so little beyond their expectations ; as also at their own *jests ;* and in this case it is manifest, that the passion of laughter proceedeth from a *sudden conception* of some *ability* in *himself* that laugheth. Also men laugh at the *infirmities* of others, by comparison wherewith their own abilities are set off and illustrated. Also men laugh at *jests*, the *wit* whereof consisteth in the elegant *discovery* and conveying to our minds of some absurdity of another : and in this case also the passion proceedeth from the *sudden* imagination of our own odds and eminency : for what is else the recommending of ourselves to our own good opinion, by comparison with another man's infirmity or absurdity ? For when a jest is broken upon ourselves, or friends of whose dishonour we participate, we never laugh thereat. I may therefore conclude that the passion of laughter is nothing else but *sudden glory* arising from some sudden *conception* of some *eminency* in ourselves, by *comparison* with the *infirmity* of others, or with our own formerly : for men laugh at the follies of themselves past, when they come suddenly to remembrance, except they bring with them any present dishonour. It is no wonder therefore that men take heinously to be laughed at or derided, that is triumphed over. Laughter *without offence* must be at absurdities and infirmities *abstracted* from persons, and where all the company may laugh together : for laughing to one's self putteth all the rest into jealousy and examination of themselves. Besides, it is in vain glory, and an argument of little worth, to think the infirmity of another sufficient matter for his triumph."[17]

Elsewhere, Hobbes, writing on the same subject, says : " ' Sudden glory ' is the passion which maketh those ' grimaces ' called ' laughter ' ; and is caused either by some sudden act of their own that pleaseth them or by the apprehension of some deformed thing in another by comparison whereof they suddenly applaud themselves. And it is incident most to them that are conscious of the fewest abilities in themselves ; who are forced to keep themselves in their own favour by observing the imperfections of other men. And therefore much laughter at the defects of others is a sign of pusillanimity. For of great minds one of the proper works is to help and free others from scorn, and compare themselves only with the unstable."[18]

Now, here, although I do not claim that we have a perfect verbal statement of the exhaustive definition of laughter, I do maintain, in opposition to most Anglo-Saxon critics and thinkers, that we have an exhaustive definition, because—and these are facts overlooked by all Anglo-Saxon critics of the great philosopher—in Hobbes's explanation, not only is the old field of the ancients retained, but it is greatly extended to include both the series of laughs which are subjective, all the laughs which are objective, and, in addition, a satisfactory reason why laughter can offend, and why some people laugh excessively.

It is characteristic of the Anglo-Saxon critics of Hobbes, that they consistently shirk the explanation of two aspects of laughter—its subjective aspect and its sting. They withdraw the sting on the one hand by saying that men do not laugh from any feeling of superiority, and then, when they are obliged to admit that laughter can and does offend when it is directed against one, they are naturally at a loss to account for the offence. Some of them, including the Frenchman, Bergson, as we have seen, actually take the sting for granted without attempting to explain it.

Laughter is self-glory. So we can now understand why a person can laugh apparently at nothing, that is to say, unprovoked by any external stimulus, or the memory of any external stimulus. Not one of the men in the first section (including, of course, Bergson), and hardly any already quoted above in the second section, thought of this kind of laugh. We can now also understand all those laughs in which there is definite outside provocation ; for, although Hobbes quite unnecessarily limits the series of these external stimuli, those externally provoked laughs not mentioned by him are, as I hope to show, implicit in his two words " self-glory."

If, therefore, Hobbes's definition of laughter has hitherto been found one-sided and inadequate, I suggest that it is owing to the fact that most critics and writers have themselves deliberately limited it.

Instantly angered by the uncharitable and " selfish "
appearance of the words " self-glory," they gave the
definition no further thought and condemned it.

And yet, with Hobbes's definition of laughter before
us, we can understand so much that was obscure before.
We can now see why the schoolboy, standing stripped
in the sunlight on a sandy shore, laughs and laughs
heartily—at nothing ! We can see why a young girl,
knowing herself to be faultlessly attired, will laugh
at the most inadequate provocation. Why the same
young girl will laugh with sincere and convincing
heartiness at the clumsiest remark made by the hand-
some young man who admires her, and will hardly
notice the profound witticism of the plain man who
has apparently not noticed her. Nothing said by
Bergson gets anywhere near explaining such laughs as
these. There is not, in fact, an example I have given
which cannot be explained by Hobbes's definition.

But this is not all ; for Hobbes's explanation also
clears up the mystery about the offensive character of
laughter when it is directed against one—a mystery
carefully ignored not only by Bergson but also by all
those who oppose Hobbes—and it gives us a most
important and valuable hint concerning the kind of
people who laugh most. This last contribution to the
subject alone sets Hobbes head and shoulders above
most moderns in the matter of psychological insight.
But I am anticipating, and must now first complete
this brief history of thought on the subject.

Spinoza, who regarded the true philosopher as a
man " who in truth finds nothing worthy of hatred,
laughter, or contempt,"[19] was not so clear as Hobbes,

and I believe his confusion arose from the same cause as that which accounts for the confusion of most modern writers on laughter. He felt, what Hobbes saw—that there are many other kinds of laughter besides that which results from a comparison between oneself and another—and yet he did not know how to include the laughter that is not the outcome of a comparison, with the laughter that is. It is the supreme merit of Hobbes's term " self-glory," that it embraces both the kinds of laughter that result from the laugher's comparison (whether conscious or unconscious) of himself with another, and the kinds of laughter that arise without any antecedent comparison. But it is surely not difficult to see that when no such all-embracing term springs to one's mind, some confusion is likely to arise, by the very effort one makes to keep these two distinct kinds of laughter apart.

Thus, although Spinoza saw quite clearly that " derisive laughter comes from the pleasure we feel at conceiving the presence of a quality we despise in an object we dislike," and although he admits that " a man hates what he laughs at,"[20] he very naturally feels that this does not by any means cover all laughter. We know, in fact, that it covers but very few kinds of laughter. He, therefore, finds it necessary to distinguish between the laughter which is derisive and the laughter which Voltaire regarded as pure " joyfulness," and says : " We distinguish between mockery and laughter ; for laughter and merriment are nothing but joy, and therefore, provided they are not excessive, are in themselves good."[21]

This distinction has, of course, delighted the hearts of modern Anglo-Saxon opponents of Hobbes. But, as a matter of fact, it is the result of confusion. To say " we distinguish mockery from laughter " (for the phrase extended really means " we distinguish the laughter of mockery from *pure* laughter ") is about as sensible as to say " we distinguish oak from wood." The laughter of mockery is only one of the many kinds of laughter. If, however, you have no all-embracing definition of laughter, and no exhaustive explanation of it as an expression called upon to do duty on innumerable and varied occasions, you are compelled to make these invidious distinctions, which lead only to confusion.

To those who claim that I have no right to extend Spinoza's sentence as I have extended it, I would retort that it can have no other meaning. It must mean that there is a distinction between the laughter of mockery and pure laughter, which, according to Spinoza, is joy, and only joy. To say that mockery as mockery is distinct from laughter, would either be to state a mere platitude, or else again to be guilty of confusion ; for everybody knows there is some mockery in some laughter. As for the implicit " pure laughter," contained in Spinoza's distinction, I shall have more to say later. Suffice it for the present to observe that, as a Jew, he was bound to know of laughter as this " pure " joy, unadulterated by any comparison. It is only surprising that, in trying to distinguish this laughter from the laughter resulting from a comparison, he did not see the beauty and simplicity of Hobbes's synthetical phrase " self-glory "—more especially as he most probably had access to Hobbes when he was writing his *Ethics*.

Swift, who knew that " men laugh at one another's cost," recognised the power of laughter as a weapon and as a lash ;[22] but he, too, seems to have been unable to find room in his explanation for more than the laughter which results from a comparison.

He was followed by Addison, who said : " I am afraid I should appear too abstracted in any speculations, if I show that when a man of wit makes us laugh, it is by betraying some oddness or infirmity in his own character, or in the representation which he makes of others, and that when we laugh at a brute or even at an inanimate thing, it is at some action or incident that bears a remote analogy to any blunder, or absurdity in reasonable creatures."[23]

All this is true and covers a vast number of instances of the laughable ; but it is very much inferior to Hobbes's explanation. There seems, however, to have been an excess in Addison's day of the kind of laughter which results from a merely physical comparison, or at least of a comparison involving joy over another's misfortune (*Schadenfreude*), and Addison acknowledges this. He speaks of the sort of men called " Whims and Humorists," who are always playing practical jokes on their guests, to create a laugh,[24] and we gather that practical joking, for the provocation of laughter, was as popular among the cultivated in the eighteenth century as it is now among the working-classes, school-boys of all classes, the Chinese and savages.

It was said to have been Montesquieu's opinion that laughter was born of pride and vanity,[25] while his friend, Lord Chesterfield, in his *Letters to his Son*, evidently influenced by the too obviously low origin of laughter, as revealed by the mirth of the period, wished to proscribe laughter from the gamut of human expressions.

" Frequent laughter," he wrote, " is the characteristic of folly and ill-manners : it is the manner in which the mob expresses their silly joy at silly things. . . . In my mind there is nothing so illiberal, and so ill-bred, as audible laughter. True wit, or sense, never yet made anybody laugh, they are above it ; they please the mind, and give cheerfulness to the countenance. But it is low buffoonery, or silly accidents, that always excite laughter ; and that is what people of sense and breeding should show themselves above. A man's going to sit down in the supposition that he has a chair behind him, and falling down upon his breech for want of one, sets a whole company laughing, when all the wit in the world would not do it ; a plain proof, in my mind, how low and unbecoming a thing laughter is. . . . I am neither of a melancholy nor a cynical disposition, and am as willing and as apt to be pleased as anybody ; but I am sure that since I have had the full use of my reason, nobody has ever heard me laugh."[26]

There is much good sense in this attitude. Most men of culture, when they are reminded of the lowly origin of laughter by the mirth over horse-play, or the rapturous jeers of the mob over some physical infirmity, may feel revolted by laughter. But it is when laughter climbs to planes less obviously associated with either inferiority in a fellow-being, or conscious superiority in oneself, that the man of culture, losing his bearings, forgets its origin, and defends it, because he knows only its obscure refinements.

Oliver Goldsmith wrote on laughter in a way suggesting that the blood relationship between the laugh over horse-play or merely physical inferiority, and the laugh over more spiritual triumphs, was beginning to be forgotten, and that the line of demarcation between the two was hardening.   He says : " Among well-bred fools, we may despise much, but have little to laugh at.   The truth is, the critic generally mistakes humour for wit, which is a very different excellence. Wit raises human nature above its level ; humour acts as a contrary part, and equally depresses it.   To expect exalted humour is a contradiction in terms. . . . When a thing is humorously described, our burst of laughter proceeds from a different cause : we compare the absurdity of the character represented with our own, and triumph in our conscious superiority.   No natural defect can be a cause of laughter, because it is a misfortune to which ourselves are liable.   We only laugh at those instances of moral absurdity, to which we are conscious we ourselves are not liable.   For instance, should I describe a man as wanting his nose, there is no humour in this, as it is an accident to which human nature is subject ; but should I represent this man as extremely curious in the choice of his snuff-box, we here see him guilty of an absurdity of which we imagine it impossible for ourselves to be guilty, and therefore applaud our own good sense on the comparison.   Thus, then, the pleasure we receive from wit turns on the admiration of another, that which we feel from humour centres in the admiration of ourselves."[27]

Goldsmith draws a distinction here, which, although it shows an attempt to raise the plane of the laughable, does not really place an insuperable barrier between the two kinds of laughter—the laughter at a human infirmity and the laughter at a mere human absurdity. These two kinds are in the same line of evolution, and it is merely a matter of breeding, education and general sensitiveness, which one inclines to. The fact that Goldsmith can no longer laugh at a human infirmity merely indicates, not that a human infirmity is never laughable, but that he personally has evolved to a stage no longer accessible to that humorous appeal.

We have only to think of the different degrees of culture—the culture of the Chinese coolie which does not make him above laughing loudly at seeing a dog run over in the street, and the culture of the Oxford don, who, quite incapable of laughing at such a sight, hilariously repeats a howler in an undergraduate's examination paper—to be able to allow for different kinds of laughter at different stages of evolution, without dismissing from the possibly humorous as negatively as Goldsmith does, appeals which leave us individually untickled. For by Goldsmith's method we can never arrive at an exhaustive definition of laughter, which, based on the belief that all laughter is the same expression, whether in the Chinaman, the savage, or the Oxford scholar, gives one explanation of it which covers both the laughter of the savage and that of the highest product of modern culture.

Lamennais is particularly interesting, because he

examined laughter from the standpoint of the expression itself, that is to say, as a facial contortion—a most fruitful line of enquiry as we shall presently see—and in this he is singularly alone. It is true that Lord Chesterfield speaks of the shocking facial distortion and disagreeable noise of laughter, but one feels that all he is complaining about is that in laughter the face may lose its settled expression of pious gravity.

But Lamennais definitely attacks the expression itself. He says : " Laughter never gives to the face a sympathetic or benevolent expression." (This is most important because Lamennais said it without any idea of the explanation of laughter I am about to advance.) " On the contrary, it distorts the most harmonious features into a grimace and obliterates beauty."[28]

Then he adds : " But whatever the reason that provokes it [laughter], if you probe deeply enough, you will find, whether the laugher admits or not, that it is always associated with some secret self-satisfaction, some kind of malicious pleasure. Whoever laughs at anybody, feels at that moment superior to him in the light in which he sees him and which excites his mirth, and his laughter is above all the expression of the satisfaction which this real or imaginary superiority makes him feel."[28a]

Except for the analysis of the expression itself, this does not take us even as far as Hobbes. But it is a useful confirmation of a certain part of Hobbes's explanation, and when we add to it a fresh factor provided by Stendhal, who hints that in order to laugh at a person, we must in some way feel that we have reasons to look up to him or at least to respect him (either as competitors in the same field or what not), we seem to be drawing nearer to our goal, the apt and brief statement of the exhaustive definition.

" I must," says Stendhal, " be able to feel a certain amount of respect for the person at whose expense I am expected to laugh."[29] This probably explains the difficulty most men experience in finding women comic on the stage (there are far fewer women comedians than men), it also explains why nobody laughs at a child or a horse falling. We feel too remote from them, in any case, to be tickled by any mishap that overtakes them. Their misfortune in the race does not give us a better chance in any way.

A good deal of what has gone before in this section is summed up in two or three remarks of Darwin's on laughter, and in reading them we should bear in mind not only what a cautious and painstaking thinker, but also what a very careful observer he was. What is more, he knew the animal world, and took every opportunity of collecting information about it.

After admitting what few stubborn defenders of the " innocence " of laughter will ever admit, that " the subject is extremely complex," Darwin tells us that " something incongruous or unaccountable, exciting surprise and *some sense of superiority** in the laugher, who must be in a happy frame of mind, seems to be the commonest cause [of laughter]."[30]

He also carefully discusses the expression itself, argues very cogently that " no abrupt line of demarcation can be drawn between the movement of the features during the most violent laughter and a very

* The italics are mine.—A.M.L.

faint smile,"[31] but, just as Cicero and Ribot gave up the definition of laughter as impracticable, so Darwin gives up the task of explaining the open retracted mouth, and the raising of the upper lip in laughter, and confesses that the question of these facial contortions is too obscure to be solved.[32]

Apart from giving us Darwin's high authority in support of some parts of Hobbes's explanation, this does not take us even as far as the latter. Although it covers a good many instances of laughter, it leaves a good deal unexplained, including those purely subjective states which appear, on the surface, to require no act of comparison for the generation of " selfglory." We still wish to know, for instance, why the lady who fell in Bond Street laughed. She could not have felt superior, nor could she have felt any selfglory. Darwin admits that " we often see persons laughing in order to conceal their shame or shyness,"[33] but he suggests no reason why laughter should do this. Nor does he explain why laughter can be felt as an affront, or, as Bergson says, a humiliation.

A member of much the same school of thought, Alexander Bain, argues that " the occasion of the ludicrous is the degradation of some person or interest possessing dignity, in circumstances that incite no other strong emotion."[34]

This, too, is compatible with Hobbes and Darwin, but like the latter, and unlike Hobbes, Bain does not say enough to include the laughter arising from purely subjective states, and he says nothing about the expression itself.

Professor MacDougall, although he takes a pessimistic view of laughter, argues, like Bergson, too narrowly, and excludes too many kinds of laughter to make his definition useful or interesting. He contends that laughter has been evolved in man as an antidote to sympathy with suffering, and that it arises only in situations which are mildly unpleasant, except in so far as they are redeemed by laughter itself; or in the presence of things which would excite a feeble degree of sympathetic pain if we did not actually laugh at them.[35]

This quite unnecessary modification of Aristotle's theory is so little helpful, and covers so small a field in the domain of laughter, that I should not have included it had it not been for the reputation of its author.

Strange to say, Professor Lloyd-Morgan comments quite favourably on this view of MacDougall's and suggests a modification of it which is equally inadequate. He says : " There is, however, probably an element of truth (if not the whole truth) in the view that laughter is a protective reaction which shields us from the depressing influence of the shortcomings of our fellow men—even when they jest. As pity softens the primitive callousness of laughter, so does laughter in turn relieve us from the depression which stupidity, for example, engenders."[36]

Thus, almost at the end of our enquiries, we still find ourselves wanting, if not an exhaustive definition, at least a verbal recasting of Hobbes's definition which, if possible, will cover the explanation of the facial contortions of laughter. For, I take it, that all this while the reader has been remembering the thirty-two examples of laughter I gave in Chapter I and has been trying to make all of them fit the definitions I have been quoting.

Now I contend that we should still be wanting this verbal recasting of Hobbes's definition had not a London medical man, Dr. G. T. Wrench, hinted at a very good and useful one by suggesting the words " laughter is the expression of superior adaptation."[37]

These are much better words than Hobbes's, because, while the latter do not clearly cover the laughter of the lady who fell in Bond Street, or the laughter of the man who loses his hat in the wind, the former, as we shall see, cover both these and every example of laughter that can possibly be made to fit Hobbes's definition. In fact, they cover every one of the examples I have given or have been able to find in life and in the literature of laughter.

We laugh when we feel that our adaptation to life is superior. It may be a purely subjective state, unprovoked by any external object, (Hobbes's self-glory covers this, too), or it may be a state of mind excited by a comparison, as when we laugh at a schoolboy howler. Or it may be a bluff laugh, that is to say, pretended expression of superior adaptation when one is really feeling inferior.

The factor of a sense of superiority in laughter has, as we have seen, always been admitted by the more enlightened critics and thinkers ; but naturally and rightly their opponents refused to accept it as a universal cause of laughter, because as long as it suggested superiority over *somebody* or something (which is distasteful to most modern people) and the factor of superiority remained in many instances difficult to find, or so completely hidden that it was thought to be completely absent, this factor was not held to be as universal as was alleged.   The moment, however, the prime factor in laughter is seen to be the sense of superior adaptation, we find that, while the more penetrating thinkers (those who have always held that superiority of some kind was implicit in all laughter) are vindicated, their opponents are defeated owing to the unlimited kinds of laughter that are covered by the state of superior adaptation.

As Professor Lloyd-Morgan put it, when combating the old plea for superiority in laughter, " as a factor in a particular type of laughter, this exultation over others and the accompanying self-exultation may be accepted ; as a comprehensive theory of laughter, it can hardly pass muster.   Not all exultation over inferiors is of the order of laughter, not all laughter is of the order of self-exultation."[38]

Quite true !   But the learned Professor is probably thinking of the purely subjective element in innumerable occasions for laughter—the euphoria of healthy children, of healthy adults ; the cases of bluff laughter —the lady in Bond Street, the man who loses his hat in the wind ; and the cases of laughter over mere surprises, incongruities or absurdities, where no conscious superiority enters into the matter at all, but which, as I shall presently show, are covered by superior adaptation.

The vague sense of superior adaptation in the girl who knows herself to be perfectly dressed, need not necessarily involve any definite image of someone else

63

wearing inferior clothes. Careful analysis might actually reveal that when she showed an abnormal readiness to laugh at anything and everything she was not even confusedly thinking of herself either yesterday or last year when she was less well dressed ; but merely that she felt exalted and was conscious that her partner was looking at her intently and with keen approval. On the same principle the schoolboy who laughs apparently at nothing on the sandy beach in the sun may or may not have a vague recollection of himself the day before, sweating over a desk—that is to say, ill-adapted. Preceding these laughs, therefore, there may be no conscious or even unconscious comparison between the laugher and another person, or even between the laugher and his late self, but simply an unusual feeling of well-being and happiness.

Thus the fear and trembling felt by most writers on laughter, lest the thing they prize so highly should be given a priggish interpretation, which would be un-Christian besides being too limited, is appeased by the re-wording of Hobbes's definition, suggested by Dr. Wrench's brief remarks on laughter.

But before proceeding to test this definition in connection with my example, something must now be said about the expression of laughter itself, which is not dealt with by Dr. Wrench, though, strange to say, the wording of Hobbes's definition suggested by his remarks covers what seems to be the correct interpretation of that also.

CHAPTER IV

EXCEPT for Hobbes's explanation in *Human Nature*, we are still without any hint of the reason why laughter may and often does offend—why, as Bergson puts it, " it intimidates by humiliating."

Why do all of us, including the animals, dislike laughter directed at us, and instinctively know, without ever being told, that it is offensive ? Why, in fact, do we contort our faces as we do, when we laugh, and why is this expression universally understood as one that may humiliate ?

Except for Hobbes, nobody gives any solution of these problems, although the new wording of Hobbes's self-glory covers the right explanation.

But, first of all, let us thoroughly clear up the fact that laughter can be, and often is, felt as an offence. This is one of the stumbling-blocks to those writers like Max Eastman, whose one anxiety is to purge laughter of every trace of unpleasantness. No one, indeed, has made a more valiant effort than Max Eastman to champion laughter as an innocent, charming and delightful pastime. In fact, so anxious is he about this one object, that he does not mind in the least how confused and incoherent his arguments become, provided that, at the end of it all, he is able to rise above his mist of verbiage and claim that he has done his best by laughter.

E

And what is his best? His best cannot, unfortunately, remove the sting from the action of being laughed at. He, therefore, finds himself in the following dilemma :

Having removed the sting from one end of laughter —that is to say, from the motivation and causation of the laugh—and having refused to recognise in it anything but Voltaire's "joyfulness," he is naturally puzzled to discover and explain why the other end —the person laughed at—still feels a sting.

I may say, forthwith, that nothing could be more hopelessly muddled and incoherent than the reasoning of those who thus try to refute Hobbes. Those readers who know Max Eastman's book and also J. C. Gregory's[1] will understand what I mean.

Take, for instance, this passage in Eastman which sums up at this point his arguments against Hobbes's superiority theory :

" I suspect that the reason why so many philosophers have deemed all laughter to be of the derisive flavour (Hobbes never deemed *all* laughter to be of the derisive flavour) is that they dreaded the prick of it . . . the reason why we hate to be laughed at is that we experience a *feeling of inferiority*, on such occasions, that is indeed logical and involved in the essence of the case. For no matter how truly the laughers may hasten to assure us that they are not hostile, but only happy —they feel no scorn but rather a delightful love of our blunder—still there remains the fact that we *are* inferior."[2]

Yes, but, Mr. Eastman, why *inferior*, if there is no superiority expressed in laughter ?

Why need the laughers hasten to assure us that they love our blunder, and that they do not mean to offend, unless there really is a sting in this kind of laughter, which you alone imagined you had removed ?

The complete muddle revealed in this passage from Eastman is sufficient to show the hopeless dilemma of those who would rule all superiority out of laughter.

When, therefore, Mr. Eastman continues in the same strain to speak of Hobbes's " erroneous theory,"[3] after having made it perfectly plain that he has not even been able to learn from it what he obviously does not know, one is apt to close his book on his none too ingenious or ingenuous special pleading, and to turn all the more reverently to the great father of modern English philosophy.

It should be sufficient for our purpose that a writer as anxious as Mr. Eastman is to prove the innocence of laughter, is nevertheless bound in honesty to admit that he who is laughed at *feels inferior*.   But let us hear what a much greater authority says on this subject.

James Sully, who was aware of the unreasoning fury provoked in many people by a superficial reading of Hobbes's explanation of laughter, wrote as follows :

" There are one or two facts which seem to me to point to the conclusion that superiority is implied in, if not tacitly claimed by, the forms of laughter which have a distinctly personal aim.   One of these is the familiar fact that anything in the shape of a feeling of inferiority to, or even of respect for, the laughable person, inhibits the laughter of the contemplator. . . . If no superiority is implied in our common laughter at others, how does it come about that we all have so very obstinate a dislike to be made its object ? "[4]

This seems to me to be final. Nothing could be more fair and judicial than Sully's examination of the problem of laughter, even if it be admitted that it is on the whole unenlightening. When, therefore, we bring the results of our own experience, as we cannot help doing, to Sully's support, it seems undeniable that, at least in that laughter which is directed at us, we are all conscious of a sting—a sting that is explained by the feeling of inferiority that such laughter makes us feel. And although it yet remains to be shown in what way superior adaptation is felt and expressed in all other examples of laughter—even in those forms in which no obvious act of comparison is implied or demonstrable—we may confidently admit at once that in that form of laughter (and it covers a wide field) in which the expression is directed at a human object, a claim of superiority is as a rule involved and certainly felt by the person who laughs.

Returning now to our original question *why* laughter has this effect, we find ourselves confronted by a much more difficult problem.

To say that because laughter is the expression of superior adaptation, therefore it offends, would be to argue in a circle and to assume too much. It would amount to assuming, for instance, that every creature, including some of our more intelligent domestic animals, is aware that laughter is the expression of superior adaptation, and therefore, by implication, that it makes the object laughed at appear inferiorly adapted. But how could human beings and domestic animals immediately and instinctively know that laughter is the expression of superior adaptation ?

Can it be possible, however, that, in the facial contortions themselves, there is some signal, some instinctively recognisable message, the precise burden of which has been forgotten by man, but which he unconsciously, and animals instinctively, read as a sign of superior adaptation and therefore a menace to their own adaptation ?

In the first chapter I said that, since laughter is provoked by a diversity of causes, among which I mentioned some purely subjective states, there must be something that is common to every laugh and every cause of laughter, that is to say, we must be able to show an intimate connection between the laugh of the embarrassed lady in Bond Street (example (i), Chapter I) and that of the child seeking safety in the folds of its mother's skirt (example (a)), as well as the laugh of the same child when it sees the clown belaboured by Harlequin (example (e)), and that of the man who inhales nitrous oxide (example (j)).

As, however, there often appears to be nothing in common between the circumstances occasioning these four kinds of laughter (not to mention the rest of my thirty-two examples) it seems as if we must change our ground, and turn from the circumstances to the expression itself.

Now Darwin observed that, in laughter, " the upper teeth are commonly exposed "[5]—that is to say, that in laughing, we *show teeth*. But, while we may be the only animals that laugh,[6] we are by no means the only animals that have occasion to show teeth. And, if we are convinced evolutionists, and believe that, just as sounds and expressions of anger, distress, alarm, kindly interest and friendliness are more or less alike all through the order of mammals[7] (if they were not, animals of different species would never understand one another, or man as promptly as they do), there must be some origin and parallel in the animal kingdom to our own laughter, and more particularly to the facial expression of showing teeth. Nor need we be baffled by the fact that showing teeth among animals may appear at first sight to mean something very different from what it is with us, seeing that we have long ceased to use our teeth as they use them, whether in killing prey, battle, or merely danger-signalling. Now animals show teeth, that is to say, they make a deliberate display of teeth, only when they wish to warn a fellow, a foe, or man, of the danger of pursuing certain tactics too far. The display of teeth, or fangs, by the cat when hissing, by the dog when growling, by the serpent when attacked or approached, and by an angry horse, if translated into words would amount to this : " Here are my weapons ; if you come any nearer, if you pursue these hostile tactics, or carry even the present ragging too far, I shall use them on you ! "

The teeth gleam. They are visible to the attacking or merely threatening foe. They are the animals' arsenal of weapons, its equipment for war, for survival in the struggle for existence. But weapons and equipment for war and for survival are, in the jungle at least, the chief concrete factor in the claim of superior adaptation. To display teeth, therefore, is to make a claim of superior adaptation. It may be only bluff, as when the terrified kitten displays her teeth to a collie dog or an airedale ; but at least the desperate claim she makes to superior adaptation frequently enables her to accomplish her object, which is to warn off the enemy without the danger of an actual trial of strength. True, she arches her back as well and her hair stands on end ; but her climax of " frightfulness " is reached at the moment when she exposes her fangs, and when this manœuvre succeeds, as it frequently does, and as it must have done millions of times in her line of ancestry in the past, we can imagine her intense satisfaction and her consequent attachment to the expression which leads to such hairbreadth escapes.

Now, if we have really descended from the animals, is it not difficult to suppose that this habit of millions of years, so useful, so deeply ingrained, so intimately associated with success and survival, should have passed entirely out of our gamut of expressions, should have been utterly lost, seeing that it reaches back as far as the reptilian period, before any mammal existed ? Is it not much more likely that, with the increasing use of external weapons, accessory arms—spears, arrows, bludgeons, tomahawks, etc.—the showing of teeth (like the using of them in fighting) while retaining its instinctive association, the expression of superior adaptation, should have become volatilised, spiritualised, and been transferred to all those manifold and complex situations in society in which gregarious animals either find or feel themselves superiorly adapted, or merely lay a false claim to such a position by means of bluff ?   And is it not exceedingly probable, if the expression was retained as a mere claim to

superior adaptation in general, that its original relation
to mere warfare, or the threat of warfare, should now
be completely forgotten ?

In short, is it not likely that, with the vast majority
of men, even the precise though general notion of
superior adaptation must now have become unconscious, only to have left consciously associated with
the expression a feeling of pleasure, of triumph, or
success, either genuine or feigned ?

This certainly explains the immediate and instinctive
recognition of laughter as an expression that may
intimidate and humiliate ; it is the only explanation of
laughter that can possibly account for the animal's
dislike of it ; for obviously, to the animal, a show of
teeth has not ceased to mean a show of weapons, and
if we accept this theory we have accounted for a very
important quality of laughter, which men like Bergson,
Eastman and Gregory carelessly take for granted.

It is strange that this showing of teeth in expressing
the emotions that accompany laughter, should never
hitherto have been regarded as one of the principal
mysteries connected with laughter and should never
have been investigated as a possible key to the solution
of the problem. But it seems probable that the
reluctance which most modern Anglo-Saxon thinkers
have shown to accept Hobbes's definition, which
hitherto has never had its possibilities fully explored,
has been the cause of this oversight.

At all events, if now, instead of the term " *laugh* "
we proceed to use, in regard to all the examples of
laughter I have given, the term " *show teeth* " (meaning
a display signalling superior adaptation), we shall find,

not only that it explains everything, but also that the number of further examples which it fits may be extended indefinitely.

Even the sounds accompanying laughter, that cachinnation which is always distinctly guttural —Darwin noticed that it came " from deep down in the throat "[8]—may be merely a specific variation of the hiss of the cat and of its remote ancestor the reptile, at the time of the display of fangs ; while anyone whose attention has been called to monkeys fiercely fighting, by the cackling sound they make, must have seen, on beholding their exposed teeth, the connection between their expression and human laughter, although the circumstances of each seem on the surface so different.

CHAPTER V

I NOW propose to test the definition by means of the examples given in Chapter I, though before I start it may be well to emphasise the fact that, whereas all laughter is the expression of superior adaptation, all states of superior adaptation do not necessarily lead to laughter, and also that whereas the explanation I have given of the facial expression in laughter seems to account for the origin of laughter, the definition of laughter would still stand, even if the explanation of the expression could not be sustained.

The letters in brackets correspond to those prefixed to each example in Chapter I, so that there will be no need to repeat the examples *in extenso*.

(*a*) To find safety at its mother's side after being chased, is to find superior adaptation ; therefore the signal of superior adaptation—showing teeth—is instinctively made.

(*b*) To know oneself well dressed is to be conscious of superior adaptation. Self-glory, not necessarily resulting from any comparison, is therefore felt, and the slightest provocation broadens the perpetual smile into a complete display of teeth.

(*c*) The other gods of Olympus enjoyed superior adaptation as compared with Hephæstos, and therefore gave the signal of it. (But in regard to this kind of

superior adaptation, it should always be borne in mind
that it is not constantly, at all stages of human evolution
or even at all stages of the same man's life, necessarily
expressed by laughter, that is to say, signalled by
showing teeth.   Physical superior adaptation tends to
be felt less acutely by adults than by children, by
cultivated than by uncultivated peoples, by the
educated than by the uneducated.   Thus, as Meredith
observed—and he had no idea of the theory of laughter
outlined here—" We know the degree of refinement
in men by the matter they will laugh at."[1]   The Chinaman, the schoolboy and the savage are much more
inclined to laugh at a person falling down and hurting
himself than the cultivated man, whose claim to
superior adaptation resides in things more purely
spiritual—scholarship, taste, science, etc., and who will
laugh only at things which provoke the sense of
superior adaptation in a more subtle and non-physical
manner.)

(*d*) As Bergson points out, we laugh only at the
human.   It is the humanising of the dog, by giving
him a wig and converting him into an ugly and
grotesque little man, that causes the animal to become
an object provoking the onlooker to signal superior
adaptation by showing teeth.

(*e*) The child in its stall is not being belaboured and
shows teeth because it wishes to signal that it is enjoy-
ing superior adaptation to the clown.   (The same
remarks apply here as in the parenthesis to (*c*).)

(*f*) Ignorant people are inclined to imagine that
their country, their language, their customs, are
necessarily the most rational, and therefore show teeth

at anyone betraying another nativity, another language, another custom. Moreover, to be unable to master as completely as they do something which is such a commonplace with them as their own language, suggests a childish failing and naturally an inferiority. In the first case, the very sounds of a foreign language suggest, to the ignorant, the inane gibbering of infants and lunatics, and the mob are therefore inclined to show teeth when they overhear foreigners speaking.

(g) We feel inclined to show teeth because we are instinctively impelled to signal superior adaptation to the extent of having our own hats on. (The same remarks apply here as in the parenthesis to (c).)

(h) He shows teeth, because, knowing instinctively that it is the signal of superior adaptation, he tries out of vanity to bluff you into thinking his adaptation is still superior, and thus to damp your own feelings of superior adaptation and quell your laughter. It is all quite unconscious, both in him and in the crowd.

(i) The lady in Bond Street showed teeth all the time out of pure self-defence or vanity. Although her adaptation was for the moment conspicuously inferior, she quite unconsciously gave the signal of superior adaptation for the same reasons actuating the man under (h).

(j) Sir Arthur Mitchell, who investigated this matter, quotes the opinions of men like Southey, Coleridge, Lowell, Edgeworth and Kinglake, all of whom declared that breathing the gas caused the most pleasant sensations ; often they spoke of the pleasure as being quite strong.[2] Now pleasure has from the beginning of time been rooted in feelings of superior adaptation.

(*k*) Here is a case of the liberation from the customary constraints, or rigid laws of reason and logic, and since every form of liberation is a state of superior adaptation, it leads to showing teeth. All nonsense comes under this head, and leads to the order of laughter which Hobbes, in his explanation, says arises from " absurdities " and " infirmities abstracted from persons."

(*l*) The more dignified a person is, the more he challenges by comparison our own claim to superior adaptation ; consequently the more relieved do we feel when his superior adaptation is reduced under our eyes for a moment. This, of course, does not apply to a case where we are emotionally related to the superior person by great reverence, respect or love, because then another emotion conflicts with our single-minded contemplation of the mishap befalling him. (Same remarks apply here as in the parenthesis to (*c*).)

(*m*) We fear no competition or rivalry from a horse, a child, an old woman, or an old man. They do not threaten our adaptation, consequently we are not conscious of our superior adaptation when they fall. But a child may show teeth when another child falls, because possibilities of rivalry are present. One must be very low in the scale of human evolution to feel superior adaptation on witnessing the fall of an animal. (See, however, the parenthesis to (*c*).)

(*n*) We show teeth when embarrassed, because we feel our adaptation is inferior, and we wish to convince the company that it is not inferior. (See (*h*) and (*i*).)

THE SECRET OF LAUGHTER

(*o*) The mishap to a performer on the stage places him in a position of twofold inferiority; because, not only does he cease to be master of the character he is acting, but he also ceases to be master of himself *qua* man. (See, however, the parenthesis to (*c*).)

(*p*) We show teeth only at the schoolboy howlers which we can recognise as such by our own unaided knowledge, because to know them as such through subsequent explanation is tacitly to confess that we might have been guilty of them ourselves—so that what might have been a position of superior adaptation becomes, if knowledge fails us, a position of inferior adaptation.

(*q*) We show teeth at a pun, in the first place because the repetition of similar sounding words in one sentence is, as Bergson points out, sometimes unintentional and a sign of absent-mindedness (that is to say, inferior adaptation). Alexander Bain also suggests two further reasons. In the grasping of a pun there is self-glory (superior adaptation) at having noticed the play on the words, and there is triumph (superior adaptation) over the degradation of a nobler word.[3]

For instance, in Shakespeare's *Henry VI.* (Part II, Act I, Scene 2), Falstaff and the Prince of Wales are ragging each other.

Says Falstaff: And I prithee, sweet wag, when thou art king, as God save thy grace—majesty I should say, for grace thou wilt have none,—

Prince : What none ?

Falstaff : No, by my troth, not so much as will serve to be a prologue to an egg and butter.

78

In this triple pun, grace as a prayer, is degraded twice—first by being confused with grace (a form of address) and secondly by recalling grace, elegance in form and manner.

Again in the schoolboy's reply to the Scripture question : " What does ' sick of the palsy ' mean ? " we get a similar degradation. The boy says : " It means having the palsy so long that you're sick of it."

Here is another instance : " We row in the same boat, you know," said a comic writer to his friend Douglas Jerrold. " True, my good fellow," retorted Douglas Jerrold, " we do row in the same boat, but with different skulls."

The degradation is here obviously the reduction of the noble human cranium to the level of an oar for propelling a boat.

(r) When we understand a joke in a foreign language, we show teeth with more than usual insistence, because we celebrate a twofold triumph—that of understanding the joke and that of understanding the language.

(s) We show teeth when tickled, because, as Dr. Robinson has pointed out,[4] ticklish places are in highly vulnerable and defenceless regions of the body, and the threat to them in tickling is therefore so serious that the relief from inferior adaptation, when it is realised that the threat is not serious, causes a correspondingly high feeling of superior adaptation. Moreover, only intimate associates ever tickle one, and a bodily attention from a very intimate friend is usually met with a feeling of superior adaptation. Added to this is the nervous stimulation, which, particularly in erogenous zones, like the neck, is not unpleasant, and is reminiscent (only racially so in the child, of course) of the eternal and time-honoured familiarities of sex-play, during which a feeling of superior adaptation is constant. It should, however, be remembered that all dogs show teeth when being tickled and rolled on the floor. Evidently, as Dr. Robinson points out, the state of one who is being tickled is a very defenceless one, at any moment the ragging may change to a serious menace, and showing teeth by the passive party has probably therefore been a traditional accompaniment of this play for millions of years before man appeared.

(*t*) We show teeth on meeting a friend, because we are gregarious animals, and every friend means an access of support, strength and good adaptation. (This particular example, as we have seen above, was explained by Penjon most inadequately, and, strange to say, it is regarded by Mr. J. C. Gregory as a particularly difficult test for theories of laughter.)[5]

When an enemy appears and we are in company, we show teeth—often quite irrelevantly to the conversation we are having—in order to signal to our enemy that we can be superiorly adapted without him, or her, in our lives. When talking to people in the street, if you notice a smile on their faces, or any hilarity, which seems to be out of all proportion to the matter you are discussing, you may usually take it for granted that someone is hovering about to whom your companion wishes to give the impression of superior adaptation.

(*u*) If we show teeth at a joke against ourselves, we do so only out of vanity, to convince the joker that we are still superiorly adapted, or else that we are good

80

fellows, or " good sports," or whatever the jargon of the day may be for the gregarious hero. If we are not vain, we either do not show teeth at a joke against ourselves, or else we show them out of courtesy, to encourage the joker. (See, however, (*h*), (*i*) and (*v*).)

(*v*) This is a variation of (*h*), (*i*) and (*u*).

(*w*) We show teeth at a surprise or an expectation that ends in nothing, which so many investigators have believed to be the occasion of all laughter, because, for millions of years, surprise and expectation have always meant possible danger, possible inferior adaptation. (The Jack-in-the-box is the classical toy of this kind of comedy.) When, therefore, the surprise or expectation turns out to be harmless, or nothing, we rise suddenly from a state of apprehension (possible inferior adaptation) to a state of confidence and safety (superior adaptation). This covers Spencer and Kant's descending incongruity, or the expectation that ends in nothing.

(*x*) We show teeth at an incongruity because it is the characteristic of a mad world, freed from the mental and physical bondage of logic, reason and scientific method ; and, in such a world, even if only imagined, we taste once more of the euphoria of irrational infancy (Freud) or merely of the joys of emancipation from reason (Renouvier, Penjon and John Dewey).

(*y*) We show teeth at a good nonsense picture by Lear or Bateman, because the figure or scene presented either makes certain human beings appear grotesque, or else is possible only in a world that has abolished the constraints of reason. See (*x*). (The more harassed we are by the complexities of our real existence, the more

F 81

likely we are to find superior adaptation in such scenes and pictures. Hence the extraordinary and increasing vogue of nonsense, during the gradually increasing complexities of the nineteenth and twentieth centuries.)

(z) We show teeth at mere caricature because of the reasons under (y), or because we happen to know the people caricatured, and find their least fortunate features so spitefully exaggerated as to render them abnormal, that is to say, inferior people. (It should be noted that " abnormal " always means " sub-normal " to the crowd, who never stop to ascertain whether the aberration from type may not constitute a *plus*, but always hastily conclude that it constitutes a *minus*.)

(A) We show teeth at disguises, because they have the power of making the familiar unfamiliar, so that the ascent from inferior adaptation in presence of the unfamiliar, to superior adaptation, operates as in (w) ; or because disguises transport us to an unreal world—a world of nonsense, a fairy world, or some inadequately explored world of the past, which we imagine to have been better than this (see (x) and (y)) ; or because a disguise may make a normal human being descend to an inferior being.

(B) We show teeth when others show teeth, because we are gregarious animals, among whom moods are infectious. (We yawn when others yawn. Women cry when they see others cry.) The quality of sympathy does not, as the etymology of the word implies, lead to fellow feeling only for suffering, it imposes on those who possess it—particularly the uncontrolled— every mood that is conspicuous among their fellows.

82

(*C*) We show teeth at a good ruse, a good trick, a good case of diamond cut diamond, and also at a witticism, because we sympathise, or side with the stronger party—the witty or resourceful speaker or trickster—and share his superior adaptation. (We only do so, however, in the case of witticisms, provided the point of the witticism does not hurt or offend our own peculiar susceptibilities. We laugh uproariously at a witticism that conforms with our own fads or beliefs, we hardly smile at one which exposes or assails them. I have tested this again and again with mixed audiences of men and women, by reciting Napoleon's witticism on the difference between success in war and success in love. Napoleon said : " Success in war means surrounding your enemy, routing him, and driving him from the field. Success in love means —escape." Without exception the men in the audience have always laughed at this, and the women and girls have always remained coldly silent and grave.

(*D*) We show teeth at good mimicry or imitation : (1) because of sympathy with the superior adaptation (skill) of the imitators ; (2) because of the element of deception which, however, *does not deceive us ;* (3) because, in the case of mimicry of persons, the imitation usually caricatures and therefore belittles them ; (4) because when men imitate cats and dogs, elephants, etc., they humanise the beasts (see (*d*) and (*x*)); and (5) because of the incongruity—nonsense state—of the situation : here you have a bird, or the sound of a bird, or a cat, or the sound of a cat, and no bird or cat. (See (*x*).)

83

(*E*) We show teeth in a mock intellectual way when, at a public debate, one disputant cracks a joke against his opponent ; and we (particularly the less alert intellectually) *regard the disputant who has had the joke cracked against him as defeated in the argument*, because a crowd cannot help feeling, owing to the instincts associated with showing teeth, that a man or woman against whom they are showing teeth must be inferior. Hence the trick of raising a laugh against your opponent in debate, which was recommended by the Greek Gorgias as early as the fifth century B.C.[6]

(*F*) The superior adaptation felt by most decent and normal people when they hear stories or references either frankly indecent or bordering on the indecent, is really no different from the superior adaptation felt by the savage and shown by him in roars of laughter, when confronted by a frankly obscene act or display. It is due to the release from a constraint—in this case from one of decency—and to the consequent generation of an intense feeling of freedom and probably also of primitive and infantile irresponsibility and euphoria. It is also due in part to the fact that indecent stories and illusions turn almost exclusively on bodily functions, particularly those of sex, all of which are traditionally associated with superior adaptation. Of course, Puritans who suffer from a neurotic phobia, whether of the functions of the organs of sex, or of some other part of the body, will not feel this superior adaptation, or will repress it. Reminded by the indecent or salacious story, of their neurosis, they will feel more inferiorly adapted than ever, and will not, therefore, show teeth. The kind of obscenity the

84

savage laughs uproariously at, however—for instance, to mention one example at random, that described by E. E. Evans-Pritchard in his able paper on this subject[7] —although more gross than that at which the civilised white man laughs, serves, as Mr. Pritchard shows, the same purpose in savage life. It releases the onlooker from constraints and conventions, the only difference being that the savage is often obliged, not necessarily owing to the greater immorality of his life, but rather to his greater familiarity with the sight of male and female nudity, to resort to more drastic breaches of what the European considers decency.

A number of further examples can now be added.

(G) A child smiles and laughs when it is being teased, a grown-up person does the same when he is being taunted, because each hopes by means of the bluff of showing teeth, to defeat his tormentor by feigning superior adaptation although inferior adaptation is felt. Shakespeare said : " They laugh that win."[8] Yes, but they also laugh that lose, if they who lose are anxious to despoil the victor of one of the most precious fruits of his victory—the evidence of inferior adaptation in the vanquished.

(H) People laugh easily and uproariously in a court of law or in any grave assembly, because in surroundings of great solemnity where constraints 'and great individual restraint are imposed, any excuse to break through the irksome limitations of liberty is seized with unreasoning avidity, and for a moment superior adaptation is tasted and wildly expressed in the instinctive fashion by the most silent and most constrained of those present (the spectators).   Hence the absurd ease with which judges, magistrates and presiding commissioners acquire a reputation for wit and humour. Alexander Bain noticed this.[9] (Children have a tendency to laugh in church and at funerals for the same reason.)

(*I*) People show teeth encouragingly at anyone who has just escaped a serious injury, or who has just been rescued from danger. They hope, by the principle of sympathy to bring someone who is depressed by inferior adaptation speedily back to a consciousness of his superior adaptation. Mothers do this to their children after a fall or an accident that has turned out to be trifling.

(*J*) Nothing so intrigues a whole company as solitary laughter; because until the cause of the solitary laugh is discovered, everyone present, knowing that he lies under the suspicion of being laughed at, cannot rest until he has cleared up the mystery and set at rest the doubts about his superior adaptation which the solitary laugher has raised. Hence the familiar anxious demand : " Do tell me what you are laughing at ! "

In regard to all these thirty-six examples of laughter (except those of feigned or bluff laughter), we should never forget Hobbes's careful opening statement that laughter " is always joy," and Darwin's reminder that the laugher " must be in a happy frame of mind." It is this element of joy in laughter which misled Voltaire into ruling that laughter was incompatible with " indignation " and " contempt," and he called it " joyfulness." As I have already shown, we need take no notice of the word " indignation " in Voltaire's objection; because, not only is indignation, in any case, incompatible with any form of laughter (except, perhaps, the feigned or " bluff " kind, and that is doubtful), but it was obviously introduced by Voltaire with a certain lack of candour to make his objection seem more conclusive. What is important is that Hobbes, like his critics, insists on joy always being an accompanying feature of genuine, unfeigned laughter. When, however, we have thoroughly grasped the fact that there is no laughter without superior adaptation, genuine or feigned, what could be more obvious than that joy must be a constant element in genuine laughter? No other emotion but joy could constantly accompany states of superior adaptation ; for, as Hobbes, in the sequel to his statement, points out, dejection is wholly appropriated by those states which are the reverse of self-glory—that is to say, inferior adaptation.

CHAPTER VI

HAVING subjected Hobbes's definition of laughter, in the new wording, to the test of practical examples, I now propose in conclusion to subject it to one last test—the evolutionary.

If laughter, or showing teeth, is the signal of superior adaptation, it seems reasonable to suppose that in its early history it must have been associated chiefly with the body and the physical side of life; because even triumphs and victories of the mind, which mankind could hardly have failed to score at the very dawn of human development, must in the beginning have been concerned chiefly with physical things—the discovery of weapons, of fire, of controls over natural forces, of housing and clothing devices. If we look back along our line of ascent, therefore, we should expect to find that the principle assumed above (parenthesis to (*c*) in Chapter V) is demonstrated to the hilt. It ought to be possible to show that the further we recede, the more crude and more physical are the occasions on which teeth are shown, and that savages, children, and less cultivated Europeans than ourselves, are inclined to show teeth only at the *physical* misfortunes befalling a fellow, at practical jokes, and at all cases of obvious physical inferiority.

Conversely, we ought to expect to discover that

civilised and cultivated people find it increasingly difficult to show teeth with conviction in the presence of merely physical inferiority or maladaptation—a man falling, or being punched on the back of the head, or losing his hat, or his false teeth—and that they reserve their display of teeth for inferior adaptation of a more subtle and spiritual kind—blunders in the speech, reasoning, or critical efforts of their equals, those laughable things which Hobbes describes as " *absurdities* " or " *infirmities abstracted from persons*," such as nonsense, wit, caricature, delicate indecencies, etc., and only those physical infirmities which can make no appeal to charity, such as misses at games of skill, eccentricities of dress, and acts of omission and mistakes which spoil an opponent's chances in a game of luck.

Incidentally, and apart from the evolutionary test here to be applied, we ought to be able to arrive at the general conclusion that, excluding states that provoke subjective laughter, all people tend to show teeth only at those displays of inferior adaptation which challenge their own peculiar claims to superior adaptation, or those which they have in common with all their equals or contemporaries, so that while a soldier would probably be the only one of a company to laugh at another soldier who had a strap or a buckle in the wrong place on his uniform, that same soldier would be able to laugh, together with the non-military persons in the company, if a man turned head over heels in the middle of the road. We almost expect the ignoramus to be silent while the scholar roars with laughter, and the scholar to remain dumb while the ignoramus wriggles with mirth. We simply cannot conceive of a man's laughing loudly whose peculiar or generally common claims to superior adaptation have not been in some way challenged by his environment or stimulated subjectively. Thus there must be whole series of jokes at which only engineers, or only lawyers, or only doctors, or only osteopaths can laugh—according to the specialised inferiority displayed in the point on which the joke turns ; while only those jokes can have a universal appeal, whose points turn on some inferiority which makes a universal challenge to all men's claims to superior adaptation, or whose points, without relating to any inferiority which suggests a comparison, nevertheless stimulate the sense of superior adaptation in some way.

Hence the enormous confusion that has hitherto prevailed in men's minds regarding the nature of laughter and the laughable, and hence, too, the angry protests of all Anglo-Saxon humorists, including that most confused and most confusing of all humorists, Chesterton, when Hobbes's definition is advanced as comprehensive and final.

For each man imagines that he knows of some case of laughter, or of many cases, in which no superiority, no comparison, no looking down, can be traced ; and, armed with this certain knowledge, he thinks he can undertake to prove the invalidity of Hobbes's view ; while the more subtle humorist, aware of the difficulty of including the laughter of obvious self-glory and comparison in the same category with those cases of laughter which I have called subjective, and which Mr. J. C. Gregory calls " private,"[1] gives up the enquiry as hopeless and contents himself with compiling a catalogue of the different kinds of laughter and their various occasions. This is really what books on laughter amount to.

But, just as each man in a given society will tend to show teeth chiefly at those displays of inferior adaptation which challenge his own peculiar claim to superior adaptation, and at releases from those conventions and constraints only which happen to threaten his feeling of superior adaptation, so, in the development of mankind, men at each stage will tend to show teeth at those provocations which challenge or stimulate their own peculiar claims to superior adaptation, or else those claims which are common to all mankind irrespective of time and place.

Hence, if we view mankind at a stage where only physical adaptation can be claimed, laughter or showing teeth will occur only over displays of inferior physical adaptation, and we shall expect corresponding modifications as the mind and spirit absorb ever larger spheres of interest.

But is this really so ? Does the laughter of savages, uncultivated persons and children tend to be provoked chiefly by inferior physical adaptations ?

My own view is that all of us, however cultivated we may be, retain to the end of our lives a certain capacity for showing teeth over cases of inferior material or physical adaptation. As La Rochefoucauld said—and he was speaking as a cultivated man—" In the misfortunes of our friends there is always something that pleases us,"[1a] and one has only to read a comic journal, no matter how cultured, regularly week by week, in order to discover what a large percentage of the jokes and how much of the humour, therefore, depends for its point on some form of subtle sadistic appeal. But what happens is that, by extending spiritually the range of our superior adaptations, we gradually come to think less of the merely physical ones, whereas the savage, the schoolboy, and the less cultivated among civilised races are more or less limited to these.

We are certainly told by travellers that what chiefly causes savages to laugh is some coarse practical joke, some brutal display of physical inferiority, and the evidence of this is so voluminous and overwhelming that it would be impossible to give more than a little of it.

Speaking of the negro of Loando, for instance, Spencer tells us " a fellow-creature or animal writhing in pain, or torture, is to him a sight highly provocative of merriment and enjoyment."[2]   Of the Fijians, Basil Thomson says : " Stunned by a blow, the prisoners to be eaten were placed in heated ovens, so that when the heat made them conscious of pain, their frantic struggles might convulse the spectator with laughter."[3]

In his account of the Melanesians, W. H. R. Rivers adduces much evidence of the way horse-play creates laughter among the natives,[4] as does also Jerome Dowd in his description of the negro races.[5]   " It cannot be doubted," says the latter writer, " that the people of this zone (the Banana Zone) take real delight in human suffering."[6]   M. W. Hilton-Simpson says much the same of the people of Kasai,[7] as do also the Rev. Edwin W. Smith and Capt. Andrew Murray Dale of the people of Northern Rhodesia.[8]   In fact, there is hardly a monograph by a field ethnologist that does not emphasise this feature of the savage's sense of humour.

Another feature of savage humour, which is common to civilised children, is the laughter created by the Brer Rabbit type of story, in which the tables are turned by the weaker party on the stronger, who seemed to have every chance of winning. Civilised children, as dwarfs among a population of giants, thus delight in the story of *Jack the Giant Killer*. And savages, exposed to enemies of all kinds, delight in the same kind of story, in which physical superiority is suddenly and surprisingly exhibited or enjoyed by the weaker party. Both Henri A. Junod in his careful study of the African native,[9] and A. Werner, in his description of British Central Africa, call attention to this.[10]

James Sully, speaking of savages and their resemblance to children, says : " Nothing comes out more plainly in the reports on those uncivilised peoples than their fondness for teasing, including practical jokes." And he continues : " Mrs. Edgworth David, writing of the inhabitants of Funafuti, says, ' It is thought a good practical joke in Funafuti for a girl to saw an unsuspecting youth with a pandanus leaf,' which produces a painful scratch, ' a good deal of laughter on the one side and volubility on the other is the usual result of this joke ! ' "[11] Sully gives numerous further examples.

On the whole, the savage, as we should have expected, seems to be on a plane where laughter is created chiefly by the spectacle of physical inferior adaptation, and it testifies to George Eliot's exceptional acumen and intelligence that she was able over half a century ago to detect the origin or basis of all laughter in this triumph of the uncultivated over merely physical maladaptations.

" Strange as the genealogy may seem," says the famous authoress, " the original parentage of that wonderful and delicious mixture of fun, fancy, philosophy and feeling, which constitutes modern humour, was probably the cruel mockery of a savage at the writhing of a suffering enemy—such is the tendency of things towards the better and more beautiful."[12]

Taking the Chinese as an example of a civilised people still below Europeans in culture, we find them also unusually prone to laugh uproariously at merely physical maladaptations, particularly those resulting from practical jokes. On this point European travellers in China seem to be agreed, while numerous reports go even farther, and claim that in the Chinese there is a sense of the humorous hardly more elevated than that of the savage.

We hear, for instance, that the Chinese " are prodigiously amused when a dog is run over in the street."[13] Mr. Dingle tells us " that in all ages, the Chinese find a peculiar and awful satisfaction in watching the agonies of the dying,"[14] and in speaking of the Chinese mob, he also says : " There is nothing more glorious to a brutal populace than the physical agony of a helpless fellow-creature, nothing which produces more mirth than the despair, the pain, the writhing of a miserable, condemned wretch."[15] But according to Mr. J. H. Gray, the joyful mirth at the spectacle of human suffering would not seem to be confined merely to the illiterate mob and to the vulgar, for even the judges and their officers also appear to be capable of it. Referring to the summary floggings administered in Chinese courts, in front of the tribunal, the author says : " I saw a punishment of this kind inflicted on an aged man, who at each blow groaned piteously. It was apparently a source of delight to the judge and his officers, and the face of each official was expanded by a broad grin."[16]

Such stories could be multiplied indefinitely. There is hardly a frank monograph on China that does not contain at least one example of the sort.

Stating the case with the utmost moderation, therefore, it would seem fair to say that humour in China is still on the level of the practical joke—physical maladaptation—as we should have expected it to be in any civilisation still at a comparatively low level of culture.

Now if entogeny, or the development of the individual, is really a repetition of phylogeny, or the evolution of the race, we should expect to find among European children, or the children of Western civilisation generally, just that stage of humour which we look for and find among savages and among civilised peoples below the more cultivated adults of Europe.

But although most people would be ready to agree that children, and boys particularly, are specially prone to laugh at the practical joke, at the April fool sort of humour, and at chiefly physical maladaptations, systematised records of these facts are singularly difficult to obtain. Two such records, however, do happen to have been made, one by Katherine A.

Chandler, who published her results in 1902, and the other by C. W. Kimmins, who published his results in 1928.

There were 700 test papers written for Miss Chandler's enquiry, and they were the work of children ranging from eight to fifteen years of age, whose homes may be described as those of the comfortable middle class.

The conclusion to which personal observation had led her was that the mortification, or discomfort, or hoaxing of others, very readily caused laughter, while a witty or funny remark often passed unnoticed.

The results of the tests, however, revealed, as might have been foreseen, that this tendency to see fun and the ludicrous only in other people's misfortunes was limited to the lower ages only, and became ever less noticeable as the children advanced in years.

The children of eight, without exception, described some action in which they had personally taken part, involving the idea of discomfort to somebody. The other pupils, as they rose in years, described such jokes with less regularity, although the boys, up to the highest age, namely fifteen, continued with frequency to find their good jokes in some situation in which their sisters and other girls had looked ridiculous.[17]

This is exactly what our theory would have led us to expect.

With regard to Mr. Kimmins's investigation, it is impossible, in this brief reference, to do justice to the excellence and great interest of his work. Although I do not, by any means, see eye to eye with him regarding the general problem of laughter, I find it difficult adequately to express my appreciation of the pains and industry with which he has collected his data concerning children.

He carried out his enquiries in England and in America, and each of them yielded results very similar to those obtained by Miss Chandler.

Speaking of English children, Mr. Kimmins says : " The misfortunes of others as a cause of laughter are frequently referred to by young children and form the basis of many funny stories."[18]   And he adds : " The misfortune-of-others story practically ceases after the age of ten with boys and girls. Not so funny sights of the misfortune-to-others type . . . they retain their popularity long after the age at which this kind of funny story has disappeared, and descriptions of them are in special favour during the period of rapid growth from twelve to fourteen years of age."[19]

Mr. Kimmins points out, however, that " in accounts of laughter in the home at domestic incidents, the girls' records are much more numerous than the boys'," and gives a typical story by a girl in which the whole point of the laughter turns upon her mother and father having fallen on the floor over some spilt porridge.[20]

In older children, from twelve to eighteen years of age, Mr. Kimmins tells us that " the misfortunes of others, as the humorous basis, unless concerned with the behaviour of adults, have practically lost their appeal."[21]

In American children there appears to be a greater tendency than in the English to laugh at stupidity in others,[22] and at stories of gross stupidity.   Apart from

G   97

this, owing to the fact that they have the same fairy tales and story books to read, their development in humour follows more or less the same course.

As for coloured children, Mr. Kimmins's general conclusion is as follows : " It is found that the stories which are selected by coloured children of twelve years of age are of similar nature to those selected by the white children at the age of nine. This difference of three years is maintained up to the age of fifteen years . . . the sense of humour of the coloured child is three years behind that of the white child."[23]

These conclusions of Miss Chandler and Mr. Kimmins on the whole, therefore, support the view that physical maladaptations tend to constitute the primitive forms of the laughable, and if we follow the development of humour and wit in Europe from the earliest times, we can, I think, see the gradual emergence of spiritual from merely physical laughter.

The process is naturally not always continuous or progressive. There are set-backs and fluctuations here and there, and we find gross humour still surviving in Western Europe long after the finest Greeks and Romans had expressed disapproval of it.

On the whole, however, the truth seems to be that in all that laughter which is not purely subjective in character, in all that laughter which is the outcome of a comparison, conscious or unconscious (and this is by far the greater part of laughter), the provocations which consist in mere physical inferiority always precede those which consist in some spiritual superiority, and that, with the rise of culture, the former provocations tend to die out, although they always survive among the younger and less cultivated members of the community.

It is not very useful to advance, as many writers do, the " laughter of babies and young children " against this generalisation, as if in pursuance of Wordsworth's puritanical views, we were bound, owing to the acknowledged sexual impotence of infants and young children, to endow them with every attribute of the divinity and the angels, and to argue that there is *something*, some lofty and magic quality about *their* laughter, to which the laughter of adults cannot attain. This is, of course, the most pernicious nonsense. But it is a view very prevalently held by Anglo-Saxon women, and men who think like women.

Truth to tell, as we shall see in the next chapter, there is a very simple explanation of the fact that children laugh so much and with such conviction, and so far from there being any superior or transcendental quality about their laughter, its provocation consists, as a rule, of the most obvious and most physical circumstances.

A very small infant enjoys, if it is in good health, a great deal of subjective laughter. It is pleased to move its limbs, to break wind, to throw things about, and to feel its strength. All these activities constitute its first acquaintance with " superior adaptation." It does not laugh and smile, as Wordsworth would have us believe, because its great pure mind is recalling its recent sight of God and the angels. Later on it laughs because it is able to recognise things. It looks at a book, sees a cow jumping over the moon, and recognises the animal and laughs. It is delighted at

99

having exercised the power of recognition, one of the primary and most important conditions of superior adaptation for the animal.[23a]

A young child laughs chiefly at physical maladaptations in another, or in an adult. It has to be forbidden by its parents or nurse to laugh at cripples, at lame people and at hunchbacks, just as the early Greeks needed to be forbidden by their philosophers to laugh at the deformed. It is only later on, at school and in adult society, that it develops the power to laugh at spiritual maladaptations. Then, too, it acquires its power of appreciating the fun and humour of sheer nonsense, of absurdities, incongruities and expectations that come to nothing—all on the spiritual plane. Expectations that come to nothing on the physical plane it has already laughed at in the nursery hundreds of times.

I suggest that the development of mankind has followed this same path, and that the development of the child repeats that of mankind phylogenically.

We find the early Greeks gradually learning from their spiritual leaders the superiority of refined and spiritual over merely physical provocations of laughter. We find the same course followed in Rome ; and, in the civilisations of France and England, the familiar stages are repeated.

As early as the sixth century B.C. Chilon was conjuring his fellows in Sparta not to laugh at one another's misfortunes.[24] A century later Democritus was praying the Athenians to refrain in the same manner,[25] and Aristotle who came on the eve of the decline of Athenian civilisation, enters with surprising

detail into the permissible and impermissible provocations of laughter. He deprecates the existence of
" buffoons and vulgar fellows, who itch to have their
joke at all costs, and are more concerned to raise a
laugh than to keep within the bounds of decorum and
avoid giving pain to the object of their raillery."[26]

He also refers to " the old and the new comedy,"
and reveals the interesting fact that the progress
registered in the latter consisted in the substitution of
innuendo for obscenity for the raising of a laugh.[27]

But " the buffoon," says Aristotle, " is one who
cannot resist a joke ; he will not keep his tongue off
himself or anyone else, if he can raise a laugh."[28]

Thus, in ancient Greece, as culture advanced, the
tendency was ever towards the cleansing of humour
and laughter of the provocation of merely physical or
even mental inferiority in another, and also of obscenity
and the like. And this tendency was very largely
directed by the philosophers. The fact that there
was need of this direction by the philosophers is
shown—to give only one instance—by an opinion
given by Reich, to the effect that in the Mimes and
Atellan farces which, from the first, were the most
popular of the dramatic *genres* in the fifth century
B.C., the ridicule of bodily defects was one of the
richest sources of laughter.[29]

We find much the same tendency in ancient Rome.
But probably, owing to the greater cruelty of the
Romans, the rebukes of their philosophers seem to
have had less effect in raising the provocation of
laughter to a more spiritual plane. Nor is this surprising if we remember that one of the favourite

pastimes of the people of Rome was to watch the brutal displays of the circus. Thus, in spite of the teaching of Cicero and Plutarch on this subject, as we see from the epigrams and satires of the later Roman writers, jokes were constantly made at the expense of physical defects in another, and we cannot doubt that they were considered extremely funny.

Although Cicero recognised the ridicule of personal defects as a fruitful source of laughter, he partially condemned it, because it savoured too much of the low humour of the mimes.[30] He disapproved, for instance, of the jest of Appius, at the expense of a one-eyed man, objected to wit turned against the unfortunate because such conduct is inhuman, and censured obscenity as a means of raising a laugh.[31]

In his *Questiones Conviviales*, Plutarch condemns laughter at certain defects—foul breath, a filthy nose, or blindness, for instance[32]—and tries to soften the asperity of the coarse humour of the period by reminding his fellows that jesting is always more kindly if the joker laughs at himself as well as at others.[33] But it is significant that almost all the provocations of laughter mentioned by Plutarch refer to physical or moral defects.[34]

In England, certainly, the development has been similar. The fact that Bacon mentions " deformity " among the first of the objects of laughter, and that we may trace so steady a refinement of Anglo-Saxon humour that, at the present day, a writer on the laughable would hardly be prepared even to include deformity among the conceivable provocations of laughter, is surely proof of this.

Nevertheless, as I have pointed out above, although we may see in the development of mankind, as in the development of the individual from childhood, a tendency to spiritualise the occasions for laughter, and, in that laughter which is the outcome of a definite comparison, to eliminate more and more merely physical inferiority or misfortune from the objects that raise a laugh, it remains true that probably all of us—the most cultivated included—retain till the end of our days a capacity for laughing at the cruder and more primitive forms of the laughable, and that therein we do but reveal the remote origin of laughter which, starting from its source (the animal's claim to superior adaptation in battle by the display of teeth) gradually and steadily developed into the human expression for superior adaptations in all situations.

And the fact, quite natural and comprehensible, that these situations of superior adaptation should in the earliest and remotest period of human development have been associated chiefly with physical superiority, has left its indelible stamp upon us all. This explains why, at times, it pierces the veneer even of the most cultured, and why in adult life it is not uncommon for men and women to feel ashamed of their sudden impulse to laugh. Whenever this happens we may feel sure that a cause we now consider unworthy— a physical mishap to a fellow-creature, or else a defect in him—has provoked the impulse, and that we are ashamed, because instinctively we feel it to be connected with the most primitive side of our nature.

CHAPTER VII

Having accomplished the first part of my task, which was to explain the meaning of laughter and its evolution, it now only remains for me to deal with the second part, which was to ascertain the condition men are in when they demand laughter with such neurasthenic insistence as they do to-day.

To those of my readers who have followed the argument of the preceding chapters, this second problem will appear not nearly as difficult as the first, and in solving it I propose to rely chiefly on the valuable discoveries of Dr. Alfred Adler, probably one of the most acute psychologists of the day.

In the first place, however, I should like to make the nature of the problem quite plain, and refresh the reader's mind concerning the points emphasised in the Introduction. I am not arguing that there is to-day a greater capacity for laughter, or a greater fitness for laughter than there has ever been. What, I think, can reasonably be maintained, however, is that there is to-day a more resolute pursuit of " gelotogens " (to coin a word for the occasion), a greater exaltation of humour, a more determined demand for gelastic literature and turns of speech, a more slavish worship of humorists, and hence, inferentially, a greater conscious insistence on showing teeth at all costs, than there has ever yet been in Western Europe ; and, if we wish to convince ourselves of this fact, we have only to reflect on how sacrosanct, how supreme, the quality of a sense of humour has become in recent years.

Neither in the Middle Ages, the period of the Renaissance, nor the seventeenth nor the eighteenth century, do we find this frenzied and monotonous praise of a sense of humour. We do not find men exalted or debased according to their possession or want of it. We are not told that the opponents of Luther, for instance, accused him, as they would certainly have done had they been moderns, of lacking a sense of humour. We do not find in Puritan literature, the Puritans accusing Charles I. of having no sense of humour, as they certainly would have done had they belonged to the nineteenth or twentieth century. Neither do we hear of Charles I., or Strafford, or Laud, bringing a similar charge against the Puritans. Swift, who was keen enough to discover the flaws in his enemy's armour, does not hurl this most dreaded of modern charges at his opponents ; and, as far as I have been able to study the anti-Napoleonic literature of last century, we nowhere find a similar charge flung at Napoleon, although, from the standpoint of the man of the period, he deserved it probably even more than Kaiser Wilhelm II.

Last, but not least, although Pascal certainly pleaded that saints might laugh at the follies of men for disciplinary purposes, I have nowhere come across any attempt earlier than the nineteenth and twentieth centuries to foist a sense of humour on God and Christ, who, in view of their exalted station, could, in the eyes of the modern man, hardly be left any longer without this exalted virtue, despite the adverse evidence of the Old and New Testaments.

There must surely be some reason for the enormously important place this gelotogen, humour, has come to occupy in modern life. There must be something behind its comparatively sudden elevation to the rank of a virtue so exalted that, on the one hand, the most studied modern insult is to deny that a man possesses it, while on the other hand, the highest honour that can be paid even to God is to declare that He is endowed with it.

Is it possible that, like all exaggerations, like all prejudices and prepossessions, which become exorbitant, it is compensatory? Quite apart from other evidence of a similar nature that could be adduced from most classical writers, Aristotle hints at the fact that the Greeks of his own day were hypergelastic.[1] Is it possible that with them, too, excessive laughter was compensatory?

What were they? They were men who stood on the brink of the Hellenistic period—the period of decline and decadence, the sunset era of Greek glory and prosperity.

But why should an age of decadence and decline be necessarily hypergelastic? The reader immediately thinks of children. Are they not always laughing? Do they not worship the buffoon and gelotogens of all kinds?

And yet children of all nations, who show this extreme fondness and readiness for laughter, cannot be called decadents. They stand on the very threshold of life. How, then, can there possibly be any relationship between laughter and decadence ?

Yes, but children are in a singular position. They are dwarfs in a world of giants. They are weaklings and ignoramuses in a world of strong, learned elders. They are young human beings with human pride and human arrogance, who are constantly having to conceal their mortification at defeats suffered at the hands of the giants. Their power, their will to self-assertion, their desire to prevail, is constantly being constrained, thwarted, suppressed by the Titans about them. At best, they find their lives controlled in a thousand tiresome ways. Adler tells us that all human motivation can be reduced to a general striving after superiority of some kind.[2] He also tells us that throughout the whole of its development, the child suffers from a feeling of inferiority in regard both to its parents and the world,[3] and that when this, as it were, normal feeling of inferiority in children happens to be complicated by some organic deficiency or debility, it produces a much more acute feeling of inferiority.[4]

He proceeds to show that every effort is made by the child to overcome this feeling of inferiority,[5] and that when the latter is abnormally severe, the effort to overcome it is correspondingly frantic.[6]

Even in normal children, however, the customary, or what might be called the " routine " feeling of inferiority, suffices, according to Adler, to account for the unremitting restlessness of the child, his itch to be doing something, his longing to play various parts, to measure his strength against all comers, his habit of planning his future, and his physical and mental preparations for it.[7]

But if Adler had known the theory of laughter expounded in this book, would he not most certainly have added laughter to the list of childhood's incessant activities, accounted for by a sense of inferiority?

Psychologists tell us that to make the facial expression peculiar to a given mood tends to evoke the mood itself in the mind. To force oneself to cry inevitably calls up a melancholy state of mind. To force oneself to utter angry words soon makes one feel angry. But, if that is so, to laugh, to show teeth, must also summon to the mind the mood associated with laughter —the feeling of superior adaptation, no matter how inferior one's position may be.

Who, then, most needs the constant tonic, the constant support of this feeling of superior adaptation, to overcome their haunting sense of inferiority, if not children? Who most needs to show teeth, every hour, every minute of the day, if not these weak, ignorant dwarfs in a world of giants stuffed with all sorts of mysterious knowledge?

Hence the gratitude, the slavish worship, that children offer to all those who make them show teeth. Hence the persistent cry of " Again! " after any scene, performance, or prank, that has made them show teeth, and hence, too, the almost neurotic readiness which numbers of them display to burst into laughter at the smallest provocation.[7a]

Oh, for that crown of laughter, that gift of self-glory that makes mean midgets feel kings among giants!

The laugh is compensatory. It relieves the constant

heavy downward pull of the sense of inferiority. It throws it off, or at least helps one to forget it for a space.

The mental mechanism by which all these benefits are secured may be unconscious, but the benefits themselves are real.

Naturally it is not claimed here that all children's laughter is of this compensatory kind. A good deal of it among healthy children is of that subjective kind accounted for by feelings of extreme well-being, of successful, faultless functioning, and of high spirits ; by a condition, in fact, in which the impulse to show teeth is, as it were, always on the threshold, waiting for the most trifling excuse to be indulged. But if we are to distinguish between children and adults of the same class ; if, that is to say, we are to find out why, all things being equal, children will tend to laugh very much more than adults who are as healthy and carefree as they, then it seems to me we must have recourse, for a satisfactory explanation, to the definition of laughter advanced in this book, associated with Adler's theory of the compensations sought by all those suffering from a sense of inferiority.

Think of the joy over *Jack the Giant Killer*, over the *Brer Rabbit* stories, over *Jack and the Beanstalk* ! In all these stories, a small insignificant creature performs a feat against severe odds, against a creature greater than himself. Think also of Mr. Kimmins's valuable discovery that the misfortunes-of-others stories practically disappear as a cause of laughter from among children from twelve to eighteen years of age, *except when they relate to adults*.[8]

What light does all this shed on the neurasthenic demand for laughter in the world to-day ? How does it illumine the obscure problem of the frenzied modern exaltation of humour ?

There can be but one inference.

This is a decadent age. It is an age in which, although longevity may be more general, the *joie de vivre* has undoubtedly declined. Quite apart from the millions who are acutely deranged mentally, or severely disordered physically, and who are distributed over the asylums, homes, hospitals and special schools of the land, even for those who are seen up and about, working and playing, it is an age of much secret dysfunctioning, of much hidden debility, of terrible sub-acute discomfort—an age of much conscious physical inferiority.[9] The vast increase in the medical profession during recent years,[10] the fantastic increase in the power of this profession, and the complementary enormous multiplication of patent and proprietary remedies (particularly aperients and aids to digestion), tell their own tale of unpublished, unreckoned physiological misery and desolation. Even the growing dissatisfaction with the medical priesthood and their power, and the surprising increase and prosperity of quacks and charlatans of all kinds, points to the longing felt by the population as a whole, to be rid of tiresome and sometimes distracting chronic disturbances in their systems, and to resort to any means, however heterodox, to achieve that end.

Speaking at the Annual Meeting of the National Association of Insurance Committees at Brighton, on October 17th, 1931, Mr. C. J. Bond, a member of the

Medical Consultative Council of the Ministry of Health, and of the Industrial Health Research Board, said that vast sums of money had been spent in education, on the relief of poverty, and, in recent years, on unemployment ; but, in spite of all our expenditure of time, money and energy, " to-day one in every ten of our people is too dull or sickly to earn a living unaided, one in every two hundred is, or has been, mentally afflicted, and one in every one hundred and twenty is feeble-minded. The fact is we . . . are heading, not for national well-being, but for racial decay."

He went on to say that a man now had a longer expectation of life by some nine years and a woman by some twelve or thirteen years than existed half a century ago. But it was possible to live longer and yet not to be more vigorous and healthy, and he wanted a populace which would not only live longer but would be more vigorous.[11]

There never was an age in which, on the one hand, petty, tiresome, and wearing physical disabilities of all kinds were more common among the supposed healthy members of the community ; and in which, on the other hand, there was such a crushing burden of diseased children and adults weighing down the sound and the healthy, who are the only support of the asylums, homes, hospitals, special schools and infirmaries in which all this human rubbish is housed.

But this is also an age of humiliations of another kind for man. It is an age in which man's environment has grown extremely complicated, and in which the complications themselves tend, though they are his own creations, to master him. Machinery is only one aspect of this tendency on the part of man's creations to master him. To a large number of modern people, many of the most tiresome complications of modern life are, moreover, quite incomprehensible, and therefore wholly uninteresting. Thus, it is not merely the vast multitude of the debilitated to-day who are chronically conscious of an acute feeling of inferiority. Even the minority of the healthy and the sound, caught up as they are in the bewildering intricacies of modern conditions, are also constantly made to feel inferior, if only for the simple reason that the whole of the modern world is too unwieldy, too difficult, and too vast to allow of an intelligent masterful survey of life as a whole. They, therefore, feel an impulse to escape from this complexity which makes a constant and frequently vain claim on careful thought and judgment, by taking refuge in a sphere where no thought and judgment are necessary, where, on the contrary, the first principles of careful thought and judgment are everywhere denied and flouted—in the sphere of nonsense. And it is on this account, as I have pointed out above (see Chapter V, (y)) that nonsense, as a form of humour, has had such an enormous and increasing vogue in recent times.

What could be more natural, therefore, than that this age, like the age of infancy and childhood, and like the Age of Aristotle, should be hypergelastic? What could be more obvious than that it should unconsciously desire the tonic of showing teeth to support its sinking spirits? The aching feeling of inferiority, whether from debility or bewilderment and perplexity, must be quenched, stifled, forgotten. Literary productions, dramatic performances, conversations, speeches—everything that fills the leisured moments of life must at all costs be humorous, must by hook or by crook raise a laugh, so that at least the expression of superior adaptation may be provoked, and that the feeling accompanying it may be experienced and relished. No other *genre* can be tolerated, no other *genre* is relevant even to the most serious subjects, no other *genre* is good form.

" Perhaps I know best why man is the only animal that laughs," said Nietzsche, who had no idea of the theory of laughter expounded in this book. And he added : " He alone suffers so excruciatingly that he was compelled to invent laughter."[12]

This age, our age, is an age of much secret suffering, of much hidden inferiority. It longs, like the child, for the crown of laughter, that will at least lend it for a space the feelings of a king. This alone explains the resolute clamour for humour to-day, the worship of humorists, and the ridiculously high esteem in which a sense of humour is held by all those who do not think of probing beneath the shining surface of modern life.

Watch the neurotic fury with which the average man and woman will defend the sense of humour if you attack it. Watch the persevering eagerness with which they display, whenever they possibly can, the whole of their dentition, even if it is false. Reflect on the misery of their secret lives, if you happen to know them well. Then ponder their unreasoning worship of humour as an end in itself. And, if you do not conclude that the modern craze for showing teeth is neurasthenic and morbid, if you do not suspect that there may be some truth, if not the whole truth, in my thesis, that showing teeth is the expression of superior adaptation, and that when it becomes excessive and compensatory, it presupposes a decadent and consciously inferior age, you must be prepared to account for both laughter and its excessive pursuit to-day by a theory different from and as all-embracing as the one expounded in this book.

The provocation of such a theory alone would more than justify the effort I have made in the present volume.

*   *   *   *   *   *

To resort to the factitious and transitory superiority of mere laughter is, of course, not to cure or remove a state of inferiority. It is not a solution. It is, as we have seen, a childlike expedient. But, as we have also seen, and as Adler points out, while children are conscious of their position of inferiority, they also make strenuous efforts to extricate themselves from it. They are not content with the merely neurotic compensations that suggest themselves, and among which I have included constant laughter. They make, as Adler says, strenuous physical and mental efforts to prepare themselves for the adult rôle, which will enable them to escape from their inferiority.[13]

That the whole of modern Anglo-Saxon adulthood, therefore, by their hypergelasticism and exorbitant clamour for humour, should be not merely resorting to a childlike expedient for overcoming their sense of inferiority, but should also be content to let it rest at that, and should not cast about them, as even children do, for a means to remove it as an active principle from their lives, is perhaps one of the most disquieting signs of the times.

There seems to be a danger that laughter is becoming no more than one of the many anodynes with which modern men are rocking themselves into a state of drowsy insensibility. There is a very distinct danger that it is helping to make tolerable a condition which should be intolerable and utterly beneath the dignity of adults. And that is why, in the Introduction, I emphasised the fact that there was cowardice in the modern resolute pursuit of humour. While, however, I described in some detail how this cowardice is manifested by the most prominent of our modern humorists, I have, until now, only hinted briefly at the manner in which it is displayed by the crowd.

If, however, we understand the hypergelasticism of our age, and its exaggerated exaltation of humour, as neurotic compensations for a consciousness of inferiority which is becoming every day more acute, we immediately see the connexion between cowardice and the rage for humour, and we have only to observe the look of settled hopelessness in the faces of our fellows when their features are at rest, in order to understand that when such lives have recourse to showing teeth in order to recover buoyancy, they must either, like cravens, have relinquished all other means, or else have failed to perceive that other means for an escape from inferiority are at hand.

*   *   *   *   *   *

It will seem to many that, in the course of this short

work, I have unduly accentuated *la partie honteuse* of laughter and humour.   To this charge I should like to make two separate replies.

The first is that the cause of laughter and humour is in such powerful hands to-day, is so stoutly and formidably defended, and has so much prestige and popularity, that, once in a way, a writer may surely be permitted to leave the almost routine business of praising, exalting and worshipping laughter and humour to their professional and other backers.

The second is that in this book I set out to accomplish two tasks—to explain laughter, and to ascertain the condition men are in when they laugh excessively and unduly exalt humour.   In dealing with the second part of my task, therefore, I was bound to touch on the pathology of modern life ; because, if the validity of my charge be admitted, if it may be regarded as proved, and if there really is such a thing to-day as an exorbitant clamour for laughter and humour, then a pathological condition is implicit in this exorbitant clamour ; for you cannot have excess with normality.

But, quite apart from this pathological aspect of the subject, as I am no moralist in the puritanical sense, I cannot admit that I have left laughter without a character.   For in the definition I have given of it, which allows full scope for all those laughs that spring from mere nonsense, merely subjective states, wit and mere absurdities, I have attempted no more than to do belated justice to a very much underrated English philosopher, and to rescue him from the hands of those who have grown either too soft, too squeamish, or too sensitive, to bear to think that their beloved laughter

116

could ever be associated with something so un-modern, un-democratic, and above all un-urban and un-suburban, as self-glory.

I still feel able to defend laughter as a glorious pastime, although I see in every laugh under the sun that element of self-glory which Hobbes's noble mind detected. But then, perhaps, I have not allowed myself to be convinced, either by modern legislation, or modern claptrap, that the highest object of every man's life is self-effacement, self-belittlement, self-abnegation, and, if possible, self-sacrifice. I see a higher purpose in life for the individual than that he should make himself his neighbour's servant or daily help, although I readily admit that there are millions of individuals whose one form of usefulness would vanish if they did not stand by their neighbour in this way. The whole world, however, surely does not wish to fashion itself upon the inevitable destiny of this section of humanity. In self-sacrifice for the neighbour, as in its worship of humour, I think this age has gone too far.

Therefore I see no objection to continuing our fidelity to laughter, although it has at its root that factor of self-glory so objectionable to modern taste. I do but warn readers that, in our excessive longing to show teeth there may be neurotic compensation, in which case, whether for the individual or the nation, it is high time to think of other remedies than the exaltation of humour.

NOTES

INTRODUCTION

[1] In his long plea in favour of laughter as a means of refuting ridiculous errors, in Letter XI, of *Les Provinciales*, Pascal, after quoting Augustine, Jerome and Tertullian in support of his contention, argues that saints may and do laugh at human error. "*Je m'assure, mes pères,*" he says, "*que ces exemples sacrés suffisent pour faire entendre que ce n'est pas une conduite contraire à celle des saints, de rire des erreurs et des égarements des hommes.*"

[2] Evidently the Bishop of Tasmania (the Right Rev. J. E. Mercer, D.D.) as a modern Anglo-Saxon, felt the same impulse as Chesterton ; for in an article in the *Hibbert Journal* (vol. 9, No. 34, Jan., 1911), after painstakingly purging laughter of all malice, cynicism, pride and malevolence, he tries to prove that God himself has a sense of humour.

[3] *Esquisse d'une Philosophie* (Paris, 1840, tome 3, livre IX, chap. II, p. 371), "*Qui pourrait se figurer le Christ riant ?*"

CHAPTER I

[1] *Elementary Sketch of Moral Philosophy* (London, 1850), Lecture XI, "On Wit and Humour."

[2] Sydney Smith notices this. He says (*op. cit.*) : "No man would laugh to see a little child fall ; and he would be shocked to see such an accident happen to an old man, or a woman, or to his father."

[3] References are given in connexion with the more detailed account of Voltaire's views in chapter II.

[4] See *Collected Writings of Thomas de Quincey* (A. & C. Black, London), vol. I, p. 25. Speaking of "readers not sufficiently masters of a language to bring the true pretensions of a work to any test of feeling," he says they "are for ever mistaking for some pleasure conferred by the writer what is in fact the pleasure naturally attached to the sense of a difficulty overcome." In a footnote de Quincey adds : "There can be no doubt that this particular mistake has been a chief cause of the vastly exaggerated appreciation of much that is mediocre in Greek literature."

See also vol. IV, p. 26, for a similar remark. See also vol. X, pp. 229–293, when, after a similar thrust at readers of foreign literature, he concludes : "They mistake for a pleasure yielded

NOTES

by the author what is in fact the pleasure attending their own success in mastering what was lately an insuperable difficulty."

[5] Extracted from the *Daily Mail*, January 29th, 1927.

[6] See G. J. Romanes' *Animal Intelligence* (edit., 1882), pp. 487 and 490, where Miss Romanes evidently found laughter disliked by a monkey.

CHAPTER II

[1] *Natural History*, VIII, 721.

[2] *The Defence of Poesie* (1594).

[3] Quoted from L. Dugas, *Psychologie du Rire* (Paris, 1902). " *Rien ne porte davantage à rire qu'une disproportion surprenante entre ce qu'on attend et ce qu'on voit.*"

[4] See note [1] (Introduction) and note [30] below.

[5] *Dictionnaire Philosophique* (Edition Touquet, Paris, 1822, vol. VIII, pp. 66–67) : " *Les raisonneurs ont prétendu que le rire naît de l'orgueil, qu'on se croit supérieur à celui dont on rit. Il est vrai que l'homme, qui est un animal risible, est aussi un animal orgueilleux ; mais la fierté ne fait pas rire ; un enfant qui rit de tout cœur ne s'abandonne point à ce plaisir, parce qu'il se met au-dessus de ceux qui le font rire,*" etc.

[6] Preface to *L'Enfant Prodigue* (Paris, edition, 1829, vol. 8) : " *Dans le rire il entre toujours de la gaieté, incompatible avec le mépris et l'indignation.*"

[7] *Ibid.:* " *J'ai cru remarquer aux spectacles qu'il ne s'élève jamais de ces éclats de rire universels qu'à l'occasion d'une méprise. . . . Arlequin ne fait guère rire que quand il se méprend.*"

[8] *Ibid.:* " *Je n'ai jamais vu ce qui s'appelle rire de tout cœur, soit aux spectacles, soit dans la société, que dans des cas approchants de ceux dont je viens de parler.*"

[9] *Op. cit.*

[10] *Lectures on the English Comic Writers*, Essay I.

[11] *Ibid.*

[12] *Komik und Humor* (Leipzig, 1898).

[13] *La Grande Encyclopédie*, vol. 28, article, " *Rire* " :— " *Quand un objet d'un côté est absurde, et de l'autre trouve une place toute marquée dans une catégorie familière, la pensée éprouve comme une secousse spasmodique : c'est le rire.*"

[14] *The World as Will and Idea* (translated by Haldane and Kemp, vol. I, p. 76). His original words are : " *Das Lachen entsteht jedesmal aus nichts Anderem, als aus der plötzlich wahrgenommenen Inkongruenz zwischen einem Begriff and den realen Objekten, die durch ihn, in irgend einer Beziehung, gedacht worden waren.*"

[15] This and many other examples are to be found in chapter 8 of vol. II of *Die Welt als Wille und Vorstellung* (" *Zur Theorie*

des Lächerlichen," para. 99). The example under (d) and that of a plain absurdity given under (k) in chapter I *supra* were drawn from this essay by Schopenhauer.

[16] *Vorlesungen über Aesthetik*, Berlin, 1835, Part III, chapter III, p. 534. Hegel's original words are: "*Ueberhaupt lässt sich nichts entgegengesetzteres ausfinden, als die Dinge worüber die Menschen lachen. Das Plattste und Abgeschmackteste kann sie dazu bewegen, und oft lachen sie ebensosehr über das Wichtigste und Tiefste, wenn sich nur irgend eine ganz unbedeutende Seite davon zeigt, welche mit ihrer Gewohnheit und täglichen Anschauung in Widerspruch steht. Das Lachen ist dann nur eine Aeusserung der wohlgefälligen Klugheit, ein Zeichen, dass sie auch so weise seyen, solch einen Kontrast zu erkennen, und sich darüber zu wissen. Eben so giebt es ein Gelächter des Spottes, des Hohnes, der Verzweiflung u.s.f."*

[17] *Kritik der Urteilskraft* (Leipzig, 1880, book II, para. 54, p. 176): "*Es muss in allem, was ein lebhaftes erschütterndes Lachen erregen soll, etwas Widersinniges sein (woran also der Verstand an sich kein Wolgefallen finden kann). Das Lachen ist ein Affect aus der plötzlichen Verwandlung einer gespannten Erwartung in nichts.*" As an example he tells the story of an heir who, wishing to do his deceased benefactor right well at his funeral, complains that he can hardly succeed in his endeavour, as the more he pays the funeral mutes to appear mournful the more cheerful they become. Another example is a story told by a wag to cap that about a man whose hair turned grey overnight through worry: A merchant, returning from India to Europe, after having amassed a fortune abroad, was obliged, owing to a storm, to throw all his wealth overboard, and he was so grieved that his wig turned white in a night.

[18] *Essays* (vol. II, p. 452), "The Physiology of Laughter." Spencer's precise words are: "As above shown, laughter naturally results only when consciousness is unawares transferred from great things to small—only when there is what we may call a *descending* incongruity."

[19] *Letters and Social Aims*, "The Comic."

[19a] Book I, chap. IV, "Characteristics."

[20] See Max Eastman, *The Sense of Humour*, p. 186.

[21] *Revue Philosophique* (Paris, 1893, No. 8, p. 114): "*Le sourire avec lequel on accueille un ami, dont s'accompagnent les paroles affectueuses, et qui parfois les remplace, ou celui de l'homme qui parvient à la fin d'une tâche difficile, sont également la marque naturelle d'une augmentation de la liberté.*"

[22] *Ibid.*, p. 117: "*Au contraire, tout ce qui rompt cette régularité, cette uniformité, sans nous effrayer toutefois, sans nous causer aucun mal et sans faire souffrir personne, nous fait rire ou nous y dispose.*"

[23] *Ibid.*, p. 118: "*Le rire parait être la suite d'une sorte de choc*"

produit par la rupture soudaine d'une uniformité d'abord constatée et dont la persistence était attendue." He goes on : *" Le caractère commun du comique ou du risible, dans les cas les plus différents, c'est en effet l'irruption soudaine d'une spontanéité, d'une fantaisie d'une liberté dans la trame des évènements et des pensées. Le comique, à tous les degrés et sous ses formes les plus diverses, est donc l'œuvre d'une liberté."* One feels inclined to retort, that mere repetition is not proof.

[24] *Ibid.*, p. 121.

[25] *The Psychological Review* (New York, 1894, vol. I, pp. 558–559), art., " The Theory of Emotion." See also Alexander Bain, *The Emotions and the Will* (edit. 1899, p. 261) for a similar idea.

[26] Quoted from L. Dugas (*op. cit.*, p. 4) : *" Le rire se produit dans des conditions si hétérogènes et si multiples—sensations physiques, joie, contraste, surprise, bizarrerie, étrangeté, bassesses, etc.—que la réduction de toutes causes à une reste bien problématique."*

[27] See *Laughter* (English translation by Cloudesley Brereton and Fred Rothwell), pp. 8–9.

[28] *Ibid.*, p. 20.

[29] *Ibid.*, p. 135. On p. 136, Bergson says : " In laughter we always find an unavowed intention to humiliate and consequently to correct our neighbour, if not in his will, at least in his deed."

[30] The whole of Bergson's theory of the function of laughter is really implicit in Pascal's eleventh *Provinciale*. It is also implicit in Demetrius of Alexandria's advice that one should use laughter in rebukes against luxury and high living ; while in Swift's contribution to *The Intelligencer* (No. 3), written in 1728, Bergson would have found a modern treatment of the same idea, almost as elaborate as his own. Swift here speaks of satire as of something " which, instead of lashing, laughs men out of their Follies and Vices." And he adds : " And, although some Things are too serious, solemn, or sacred to be turned into Ridicule, yet the Abuses of them are certainly not ; since it is allowed that corruptions in *Religion*, *Politicks*, and *Law*, may be proper *Topicks* for this kind of *Satyr*." But in the next passage, he anticipates the whole of Bergson's theory of the function of laughter. " There are two ends," he says, " that men propose in writing Satyr ; one of them less noble than the other, as regarding nothing further than the private Satisfaction, and Pleasure of the Writer ; but without any View towards *personal malice :* The other is a *publick spirit*, prompting Men of *Genius* and Virtue, to mend the World as far as they are able. And as both these Ends are innocent, so the latter is highly commendable. With regard to the former, I demand, whether I have not as good a Title to laugh, as Men have to be ridiculous ; and to expose Vice, as another

has to be vicious. If I ridicule the Follies and corruptions of a *Court*, a *Ministry*, or a *Senate*, are they not amply paid by *Pensions*, *Tithes*, and *Power;* while I expect, and desire no other Reward, than that of laughing with a few friends in a Corner ? "

Besides, we have only to recall the way our nurses used to incite our brothers and sisters to laugh at us when we were doing anything silly or naughty, to see how thoroughly obvious Bergson's theory of the social use of laughter is. But to regard it, as he does, as the one function of laughter, is, of course, absurd. That is, among other reasons, why, although Bergson sees a sinister element in laughter, we have placed him in the section of those who have made a superficial examination of the problem.

[31] Schopenhauer, who did not make nearly such an important point of the humiliating effect of laughter as Bergson does, at least saw the necessity of explaining why laughter does humiliate, and although his explanation is inadequate, he ingeniously makes it fit in with his general theory of laughter. He says (in chap. 8 of vol. II of the *Welt als Wille und Vorstellung*) : " The fact that laughter of others at the things we do, or seriously say, offends us so acutely, is due to our recognition that their laughter expresses that there is some conspicuous incongruity between our ideas and objective reality." His original words are : " *Dass das Lachen Anderer über Das, was wir thun oder ernstlich sagen, uns so empfindlich beleidigt, beruht darauf, dass es aussagt, zwischen unsern Begriffen und der objektiven Realität sei eine gewaltige Inkongruenz.*"

[32] For a careful and reliable enumeration of them see *Le Bergsonisme*, by Julien Benda.

CHAPTER III

[1] *Philebus*, 48–50.

[2] *Republic*, II, 388 E. (Translation by J. L. Davies, M.A., and D. Vaughan, M.A.).

[3] *Ibid.*, V, 452 D.

[4] *Laws* (Grote's Translation, VII, 803c).

[5] *Poetics*, V, 2 (Translation by W. Hamilton Fyfe).

[6] *Rhetoric*, II, XII, 16 (Translation by J. H. Freese).

[7] *Coislinian Treatise* (translated by Lane Cooper, Oxford, 1904).

[8] *On Style*, III, 170.

[9] *De Oratore* (II, lviii), translation by William Guthrie (Oxford, 1808), p. 252.

[10] *Institutiones Oratoriae*, book VI, chap. III, 6, etc.

[11] *Ibid.*, 8.

[12] Plutarch's *Moralia* (translated by W. W. Goodwin, Ph.D., edit. 1870, vol. III). Book II of the *Symposiaca*, Quest. 9 (p. 237).

[13] *Les Passions de l'Ame* (edition : Paris, 1664, article CXXV) :

NOTES

" *Or encore qu'il semble que le ris soit une des principaux signes de la joie, elle ne peut toutefois le causer que lorsqu'elle est seulement médiocre, et qu'il a quelque admiration ou quelque haine meslée avec elle.*"

[14] *Ibid.* (Article CXXVI) : " *L'expérience aussi nous fait voir, qu'en toutes les rencontres qui peuvent produire ce Ris éclatant, qui vient du poulmon, il y a toujours quelque petit sujet de Haine, ou du moins d'admiration.*"

[15] *Op. cit.* (translation), p. 198. "Laughter cannot be absolutely just. Nor should it be kind-hearted either."

[16] *The Temple* (" The Church Porch.").

[17] *Human Nature* (Molesworth Edition of Works, vol. IV, chap. IX, para. 13).

[18] *Leviathan*, chap. VI.

[19] *Ethics*, part IV, Prop. L Schol.

[20] *Ibid.*, part III, " Definitions and Emotions," XI.

[21] *Ibid.*, part IV, Prop. XLV Schol.

[22] See note [30] of chap. II *supra*.

[23] *Spectator*, No. 47.

[24] *Spectator*, No. 371.

[25] This is only alleged by the compiler of a contemporary MS. on *Laughter*, and edited by *Poinsinet de Sivri*.

[26] Letter 144.

[27] *Polite Learning in Europe* (1759), chap. XI.

[28] *Op. cit.*, p. 370 : " *Jamais le rire ne donne à la physiognomie une expression de sympathie et de bienveillance. . . . Tout au contraire, il fait grimacer le visage le plus harmonieux, il efface la beauté.*"

[28a] *Ibid.* : " *Mais quelle que soit la cause qui le provoque* [laughter], *allez au fond, vous le trouverez constamment accompagné, qu'on se l'avoue ou non, d'une secrète satisfaction d'amour-propre, de je ne sais quel plaisir malin. Quiconque rit d'un autre, se croit en ce moment supérieur à lui par le côté où il l'envisage et qui excite son rire, et le rire est surtout l'expression du contentement qu'inspire cette supériorité réelle ou imaginaire.*"

[29] *Œuvres Completes*, " *Racine et Shakespeare*," chap. II, *Le Rire*, p. 23 : " *Il faut que j'accorde un certain degré d'estime à la personne aux dépens de laquelle on prétend me faire rire.*"

[30] *The Expression of the Emotions in Man and Animals* (edit. 1872), p. 200.

[31] *Ibid.*, p. 210.

[32] *Ibid.*, pp. 207–208.

[33] *Ibid.*, p. 214.

[34] *The Emotions and the Will* (4th edition, 1899, chap. XIV, " The Emotions," p. 257).

[35] In an address before the Subsection of Psychology at the British Association, reported in *Nature* (Jan. 1, 1914, vol. XCII, p. 516).

[36] *Encyclopædia of Religion and Ethics*, " Art—Laughter," vol. 7, p. 805.

[37] In Dr. Wrench's discussion of the problem of laughter in his *Grammar of Life* (Heinemann, 1908, pp. 67–68) there is a description of the various kinds of laughter, to which I do not entirely subscribe, and in which laughter as successful or superior adaptation is mentioned as only one kind among many. I suggest that all laughter is of one kind—the expression of superior adaptation. But this difference in our views does not, as far as I am concerned, detract from the usefulness of the phrasing suggested by Dr. Wrench's analysis, and I have, therefore, adopted the suggestion.

[38] *Op. cit.*

CHAPTER IV

[1] *The Nature of Laughter* (London, 1924). See particularly pp. 117 and 201.

[2] *Op. cit.*, p. 36.

[3] *Ibid.*, p. 37.

[4] *An Essay on Laughter* (London, 1902), pp. 143–144. See also Alex. Bain, *Westminster Review*, Oct., 1847, p. 55 : " Laughter is a source of prodigious moral power ; it is a weapon that can inflict pain and torture, and largely influences the actions of men." And the same author (*English Composition and Rhetoric*, London, 1888, part II, p. 236) : " To be ourselves laughed at, or derided, is a severe infliction." See also Aristotle, *Rhetoric*, II, 2, 12 : " Men are angry with those who laugh, mock or scoff at them, for this is an insult. . . . But these acts must be of such a kind that they are neither retaliatory nor advantageous to those who commit them ; for if they are, they then appear due to gratuitous insult." See also Cicero, *Oratore*, II, LVIII, who advises an orator to raise a laugh " because it lessens, confounds, hampers, frightens and confutes the opponent."

[5] *Op. cit.*, pp. 205–206. On p. 202 Darwin says : " The upper teeth are always exposed."

[6] Anxious to explain even laughter as an evolved function, Darwin, in the work already quoted, tries to show that monkeys and apes laugh, but his argument is not convincing. One cannot help suspecting anthropomorphic interpretation in these cases of so-called animal laughter. Even if it were true, however, it would only show that among very sociable animals, like monkeys, beginnings were already traceable of the same unconscious processes that have taken place in men.

[7] Darwin has a good deal to say in support of this. See *The Expression of the Emotions*, pp. 60 and 358.

[8] *Op. cit.*, p. 207.

NOTES

CHAPTER V

[1] *Works of George Meredith* (edit. 1898), vol. 32, p. 74. See also Friedrich Nietzsche (Authorised English Translation, vol. VII, *Human—All-too-Human*, part II, p. 137): "How and when a woman laughs is a sign of her culture, but in the ring of laughter her nature reveals itself, and in highly cultured women perhaps even the last insoluble residue of their nature."

[2] *Dreaming, Laughing and Blushing*, by Sir Arthur Mitchell, K.C.B. (London, 1905), p. 101.

[3] *Westminster Review*, October, 1847, article: "Wit and Humour," p. 39.

[4] See Sully, *op. cit.*, p. 180.

[5] *Op. cit.*, pp. 201–202.

[6] Aristotle, *Rhetoric*, III, XVIII, 7. "As for jests, since they may sometimes be useful in debates, the advice of Gorgias was good—to confound the opponents' earnest with jest and their jest with earnest." See also Cicero (*De Oratore*, book II, LVIII, quoted under note [4], chapter IV.)

[7] See *Journal of the Royal Anthropological Institute*, vol. LIX, 1929: "Some Collective Expressions of Obscenity in Africa. The A-Kamba," p. 318.

[8] *Othello*, Act IV, Scene I.

[9] *The Emotions and the Will*, p. 261 (note) and *Westminster Review*, p. 38.

CHAPTER VI

[1] *Op. cit.*, p. 72.

[1a] *Maximes:* "Dans les malheurs de nos amis il y a toujours quelquechose qui nous plaît."

[2] *Ethics*, vol. I (edit., 1897), p. 383. See also Alexander Bain, *English Composition and Rhetoric*, part II, p. 237: "Among Savages a drowning man's struggles will be viewed with exultant laughter."

[3] *The Fijians* (London, 1908), p. 96.

[4] *The History of Melanesian Society*, vol. I, p. 46.

[5] *The Negro Races* (London, 1907), p. 378.

[6] *Op. cit.*, p. 388.

[7] *The Land and Peoples of the Kasai*, p. 272.

[8] *The Ila-speaking Peoples of Northern Rhodesia*, vol. II, p. 344.

[9] *The Life of a South African Tribe*, vol. II, pp. 247–248.

[10] *The Natives of British Central Africa*, p. 233.

[11] *Op. cit.*, p. 229.

[12] Essays (edit. London, 1884), *German Wit: Heinrich Heine*, pp. 82–83.

NOTES

[13] Martin Armstrong : *Laughing*, p. 24.

[14] *Across China on Foot*, by E. J. Dingle (London, 1911), p. 93.

[15] *Ibid.*, p. 344.

[16] J. H. Gray, *China*, vol. I, p. 53.

[17] *Century Magazine* (New York, Oct., 1902), " The Sense of Humour in Children," pp. 959–960.

[18] *The Springs of Laughter*, p. 95.

[19] *Ibid.*

[20] *Op. cit.*, p. 102.

[21] *Op. cit.*, p. 106–107.

[22] *Op. cit.*, p. 133.

[23] *Op. cit.*, p. 168.

[23a] Mr. Chesterton in his article on " Humour " in vol. II of the 14th edition of the *Encyclopædia Britannica*, uses the same example for a discussion of child laughter. But, although he has no lucid theory of his own, he is so anxious to express his hatred of the kind of theory propounded by Hobbes, that, as usual, he entirely caricatures the case of his opponent, and thereby merely reveals his own confusion and prejudice. He says, referring to the child's laughter at the cow jumping over the moon : " It is very hard for the most imaginative psychologist to believe that, when a baby bursts out laughing at the image of a cow jumping over the moon, he is really finding pleasure in the probability of the cow breaking her leg when she comes down again." Hobbes would, of course, never have maintained anything so far-fetched or foolish as Mr. Chesterton's suggested interpretation. But, unlike Mr. Chesterton, Hobbes would have claimed that there are occasions when a child can laugh cruelly. And the evidence given in chapter VI proves this to be both possible and common.

[24] *Diogenes Laertius* (1–70, translated by R. D. Hicks, M.A.). Cleobulus also has a stricture against laughter at other people's expense. He says : " When men are being bantered, do not laugh at their expense, or you will incur their hatred " (*Diogenes Laertius*, I, 93). But here the stricture is inspired less by kindliness and good taste than by plain utilitarianism.

[25] Mary A. Grant, *The Ancient Rhetorical Theories of the Laughable* (Madison, 1924), p. 37.

[26] *Ethics* (translated by H. Rackham, M.A.), book IV, VIII, 3.

[27] *Ibid.*, IV, VIII, 6.

[28] *Ibid.*, IV, VIII, 10.

[29] Mary A. Grant (*op. cit.*, p. 90).

[30] *De Oratore*, II, LVIII and LIX. (Translation given *supra*.)

[31] *De Oratore*, II, LX. Cicero repeats the joke of Appius as follows : " I will sup with you, said he, to my friend Sextius, who has but one eye, for I see there is a vacancy for me." In chap. LVIII Cicero says, " It is indecent to insult the miserable," and warns the orator against falling into the farcical character in

chap. LIX. Both in chaps. LIX and LX he condemns obscenity.
[32] *Symposiaca*, book II, quest. I, 9. (For translation and edition see note [12], chap. III *supra*.)
[33] *Ibid.*, quest. I, 12.
[34] *Ibid.*, quest. I, 9.

CHAPTER VII

[1] *Ethics*, IV, VIII, 4.
[2] *Praxis und Theorie der Individualpsychologie* (3rd edition), p. 5. " *Die eingehendste Betrachtung ergibt nun, dass wir die seelischen Bewegungen aller Art am besten verstehen können, wenn wir als ihre allgemeinste Voraussetzung erkannt haben, dass sie auf ein Ziel der Ueberlegenheit gerichtet sind.*"
[3] *Ibid.*, p. 9 : " *Dem Kinde haftet während der Ganzen Zeit seiner Entwicklung ein Gefühl der Minderwertigkeit in seinem Verhältnis zu den Eltern und zur Welt an.*"
[4] *Ibid.*, p. 12 : " *Der Besitz hereditär mindewertiger Organe, Organsysteme und Drüsen mit innerer Sekretion für das Kind in den Anfängen seiner Entwicklung eine Position schaffe, in der das sonst normale Gefühl der Schwäche und Unselbständigkeit ganz ungeheuer vertieft wird und sich zu einem tief empfundenen Gefühl der Minderwertigkeit auswächst.*"
[5] *Ibid.*, pp. 13–15.
[6] *Ibid.*, chapter 4, pp. 22–25.
[7] *Ibid.*, p. 9 : " *Dieses Gefühl der Minderwertigkeit erzeugt die beständige Unruhe des Kindes, seinem Betätigungsdrang, sein Rollensuchen, sein Kräftemessen, sein Vorbauen in die Zukunft und seine körperlichen und geistigen Vorbereitungen.*"
[7a] In regard to this, we should remember Hobbes's words in the *Leviathan*, where, speaking of laughter, he says : " And it is incident most to them that are conscious of the fewest abilities in themselves." To have made this remark, so prophetic of the discoveries of our advanced twentieth-century psychology, shows Hobbes to have been a psychologist of unusual power and perspicacity.
[8] See chapter VI *supra*, note [21].
[9] See Spencer's *Education* (edit. 1902, p. 13) : " Look around and see how many men and women [you] can find in middle or later life who are thoroughly well. Only occasionally do we meet with an example of vigorous health continued to old age ; hourly we meet with examples of acute disease, chronic ailment, general debility, premature decrepitude." The fact that Spencer was able to write this in 1861, seventy-one years ago, shows how long this state of prevailing debility has existed and has been noticeable to the observer.
[10] In 1881 there were 23,275 medical practitioners, and the

population of the British Isles was 35,241,482. In 1901 the number of medical practitioners had risen to 36,912 to a population that had grown only to 41,976,827. In 1921 there were 45,408 doctors to a population that had grown to 47,146,506, and in 1926 there were 52,614 doctors to a population of only 48,190,000. Commenting on this the editor of the *British Medical Journal* says: " These figures show a steady increase in the ratio of doctors to population, which was accelerated during the years following the War. The number of registered practitioners at the end of 1920 was nearly double the number at the end of 1881, but the population of Great Britain and Ireland within that period of forty years only increased by about 34 per cent. There is now considerably more than one name in the *Medical Register* to every thousand of population." (*Brit. Med. Journal*, Sept. 6, 1930, p. 350.) The ominous fact is that, with all this increase in the number of medical practitioners, the national health steadily declines.

[11] Reported in the *Sunday Times*, Oct. 18th, 1931.

[12] *Will to Power* (Authorised English Translation by A. M. Ludovici), vol. I, p. 74. And this explains the " pure " laughter of which Spinoza spoke (see chap. III *supra*). By this " pure " laughter I can only think Spinoza meant what I call subjective laughter, the laughter which appears to have no provocation from outside, but of which the Jew would be capable, because in Spinoza's age he had suffered so much.

[13] See note [7] *supra*.

INDEX

ADDISON, did not think laughter harmless, 42 ; his view of laughter,
54
ADLER, Alfred, his psychological discoveries, 104 ; on the restlessness
of children, 107, 108 ; on conscious inferiority of children, 114
AFRICAN NATIVES, what they laugh at, 93
ARISTOTLE, did not think laughter harmless, 42, 44 ; his discussion
of laughter in the *Poetics*, 43, 44 ; his definition of wit, 44 ; 47,
61 ; on permissible and impermissible provocations of laughter,
100, 101 ; hints that the Greeks of his day were hypergelastic,
106 ; on the usefulness of raising a laugh in debates, 125
AUGUSTINE, argued that saints laugh at human error, 118
AVORY, Mr. Justice, rebukes laughter against the legal profession, 23
BACON, Lord, his jejune definition of laughter, 27, 33 ; on laughter
at deformity, 102

BAIN, Alexander, did not think laughter harmless, 42 ; his view of
laughter, 60 ; on puns, 78 ; on the facile reputation for wit
acquired by august personages, 86 ; on the power of laughter,
124
BATEMAN, his caricatures, 25, 81
Battle of the Frogs and Mice, 17
BENDA, Julien, on Bergsonism, 122
BENSON, Sir Frank, an unfortunate accident to, causes laughter, 21,
22
BERGSON, sees no mystery in laughter, 27 ; his view of laughter, 36,
37, 38, 39, 40, 46 ; 50, 51, 61, 65, 72, 75 ; on puns, 78 ; on
intention to humiliate in laughter, 121 ; 122
BIBLE, the, no joke in, 10
BOND, C. J., of the Ministry of Health, on modern decadence, 111
BYRON, saw no mystery in laughter, 27 ; his view of laughter, 34

CARICATURES, reason for laughter over, 82
CARLYLE, regarded laughter as innocent, 27 ; his pretentious and
shallow *Sartor Resartus*, 34 ; his view of laughter, 34 ; his view
the most inadequate and false of all, 41
CHARLES I., not accused of lack of sense of humour by the Puritans,
105

I   129

INDEX

INDEX

INDEX

INDEX

INDEX

PRINTED IN GREAT BRITAIN BY
MACKAYS LIMITED, CHATHAM